Sunday School BASICS

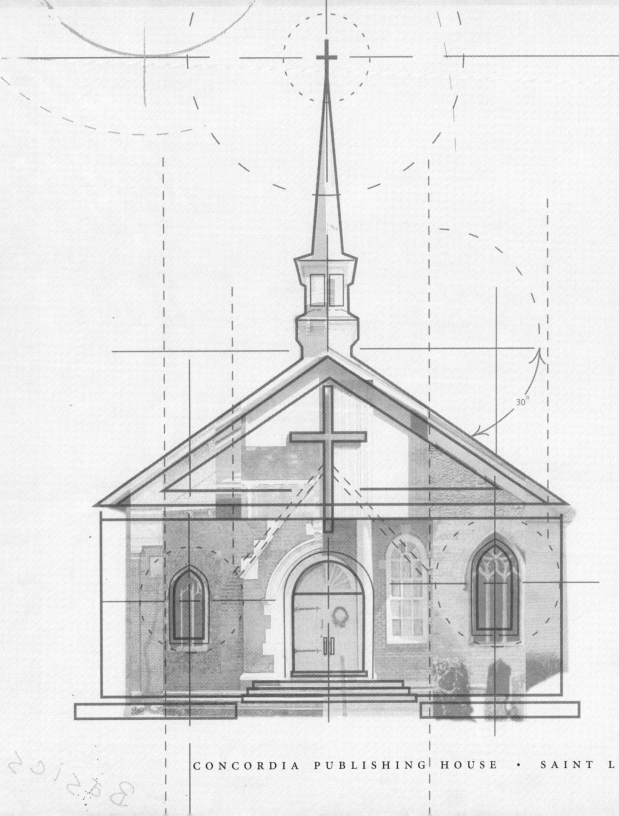

CONCORDIA PUBLISHING HOUSE • SAINT LOUIS

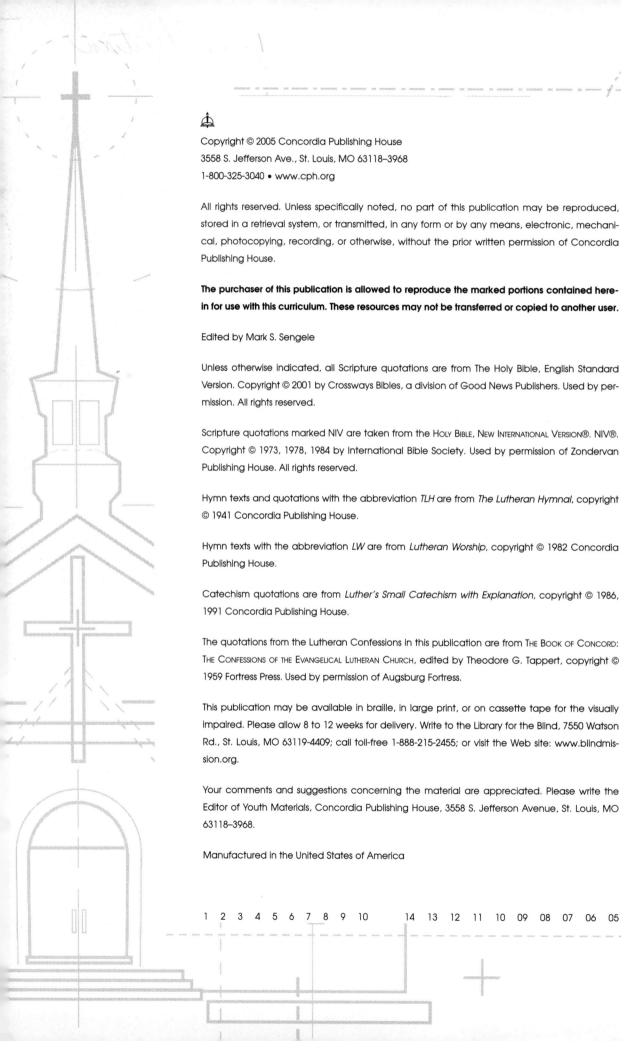

Edited by Mark S. Sengele

Unless otherwise indicated, all Scripture quotations are from The Holy Bible, English Standard Version. Copyright © 2001 by Crossways Bibles, a division of Good News Publishers. Used by permission. All rights reserved.

Scripture quotations marked NIV are taken from the HOLY BIBLE, NEW INTERNATIONAL VERSION®. NIV®. Copyright © 1973, 1978, 1984 by International Bible Society. Used by permission of Zondervan Publishing House. All rights reserved.

Hymn texts and quotations with the abbreviation *TLH* are from *The Lutheran Hymnal*, copyright © 1941 Concordia Publishing House.

Hymn texts with the abbreviation *LW* are from *Lutheran Worship*, copyright © 1982 Concordia Publishing House.

Catechism quotations are from *Luther's Small Catechism with Explanation*, copyright © 1986, 1991 Concordia Publishing House.

The quotations from the Lutheran Confessions in this publication are from THE BOOK OF CONCORD: THE CONFESSIONS OF THE EVANGELICAL LUTHERAN CHURCH, edited by Theodore G. Tappert, copyright © 1959 Fortress Press. Used by permission of Augsburg Fortress.

This publication may be available in braille, in large print, or on cassette tape for the visually impaired. Please allow 8 to 12 weeks for delivery. Write to the Library for the Blind, 7550 Watson Rd., St. Louis, MO 63119-4409; call toll-free 1-888-215-2455; or visit the Web site: www.blindmission.org.

Your comments and suggestions concerning the material are appreciated. Please write the Editor of Youth Materials, Concordia Publishing House, 3558 S. Jefferson Avenue, St. Louis, MO 63118–3968.

Manufactured in the United States of America

1 2 3 4 5 6 7 8 9 10   14 13 12 11 10 09 08 07 06 05

Sunday School

table of contents

BASICS

Introduction

The History of Sunday School

Sunday School Basics is a book about fundamentals. This book covers the basic things that you need to know about Sunday School in order to assist in carrying out its mission in the Church today. The chapters that follow offer wonderful instruction and advice on the fundamentals of Sunday School for Lutheran churches. The authors of each chapter are experienced leaders in the Church, people with a heart for teaching children about their Lord. The list of authors includes pastors, teachers, directors of Christian education, and church musicians who rolled up their sleeves and got involved in Sunday School in their own parishes and beyond. What they have to say is important and useful to you as a Sunday School leader in your own congregation.

This book offers the who, what, where, when, and how of Sunday School in a practical format. You will want to find a visible home for *Sunday School Basics* on your shelf so you can return to it time and again as you serve in your congregation's Sunday School. We'll start by exploring the history and foundation of Sunday School in order to better understand its existence in the Church today.

Long before the advent of Sunday School, the importance of teaching the faith to children was a priority for God and His people. Moses and the children of Israel were instructed by God in Deuteronomy to teach His commandments to their children:

> And these words that I command you today shall be on your heart. You shall teach them diligently to your children, and shall talk of them when you sit in your house, and when you walk by the way, and when you lie down, and when you rise. (Deuteronomy 6:6–7)

Proverbs offer the wisdom to, "Train up a child in the way he should go; even when he is old he will not depart from it" (Proverbs 22:6). Our Lord Jesus chastised the disciples who sought to disperse the children who were gathering around Him, "But Jesus called them to Him, saying, 'Let the children come to Me, and do not hinder them, for to such belongs the kingdom of God' " (Luke 18:16).

Martin Luther produced a handy booklet to aid parents in teaching the faith to their children. Luther's Small Catechism has been a staple in Lutheran churches and homes since it was first printed in 1529.

The religious training of children has always been the vocation of Christian parents, who taught by example and direct instruction using the Scriptures and then the Small Catechism. The birth of Sunday School resulted from the lack of religious instruction in the home. When, how, and why did this major shift in the religious instruction of children occur?

A fixture on the landscape of American Christianity, Sunday School is a well worn institution. Since its early beginnings in the late-1700s, Sunday School found a solid place in Protestant Christianity. In its heyday, Sunday School was *the* institution for children to regularly hear the stories of the Bible and learn how God wove His plan of salvation through the lives of sinful men and women, sending His Son, Jesus Christ, to redeem a broken and dying world from sin, death, and the devil.

On the timeline of Christianity, Sunday School as a formal institution is a relatively young institution, beginning nearly 1,800 years after the birth of Christ. Its birth took place in the slums of Gloucester, England. A benevolent Englishman, John Raikes, was concerned for the many orphans and poor children running unattended through the city streets. These children were unchurched and unschooled. Raikes funded and organized a basic school which taught the basics of the Christian faith, along with reading, writing, and arithmetic.

From that humble beginning rose a worldwide movement, the impact of which the Church still feels. To understand the phenomenon of Sunday School, it is helpful to know something about the period in which it originated.

The late-eighteenth century was an age of innovation. People were religious, and their faith gave rise to philanthropy that sought to transform society. There was great enthusiasm in Protestant churches, which gave birth to benevolent societies and agencies—religious, medical, educational, and moral charities. This model was adopted worldwide, but nowhere as zealously as on American soil.

Evangelical Christians, eager to do the Lord's work, were spurred on by the fiery sermons of their preachers. The colonists left England for religious reasons and worked together to fight the Crown and for survival in the new land. Denominational parameters were not important as members of various church bodies joined together to accomplish common goals.

Many of these societies or their vestiges are still around today. The YMCA, YWCA, and the American Bible Society are but a few that still remain. However, it was in the founding of Sunday Schools that this charitable work found its greatest expression.

The first Sunday Schools, although sometimes held in a church building, were not church run or sponsored. They were organized and led by laypeople who spent their leisure time teaching poor, needy children to read the Bible, to write, and cipher.

By 1824, the American Sunday School Union was formed. It was a national program that focused on the formation of Sunday Schools and the publishing of materials for use in Sunday School. The ASSU was also proudly unionistic, containing members of many denominations. By 1830, the ASSU led a drive to establish Sunday

School in every place it could throughout the Mississippi Valley. This was an astounding goal and its achievement is evident today in nearly every Protestant congregation in America.

During the same period Protestant educational philosophy was taking shape. Common schools were formed, which met during the week, to teach the core subjects and basic morality. The focus of Sunday Schools then shifted to purely religious education. The Protestant strategy entailed so-called public school alongside the Sunday School. This model worked because the common schools of the eighteenth century reflected the general worldview of Protestant Christians (the prevailing norm in young America).

The Sunday Schools of this era shared these traits: they were led by the laity, they lacked denominational teaching, they were self-supporting, and they were evangelistically minded. Still important today, the Sunday School picnic and Rally Day owe their beginnings to the early days of Sunday School in America. These early Sunday Schools utilized the study of the Bible with a strong emphasis on morality and developed their own "evangelical creed" that partnered with the "Rules for Sunday School" in 1824.

This early, independent Sunday School movement met with resistance as it tried to assimilate itself into the various denominations. In particular, resistance was greatest among mainline churches (such as the Anglican, Presbyterian, Methodist, and others) that already had well-established systems whereby the clergy taught through their sermons and confirmation classes. With its lay character, its focus upon children, and its lack of continuity with denominational heritages, Sunday School had increasing difficulty existing alongside the various church bodies. From its earliest days, Sunday School was criticized for superseding family instruction in the faith.

Despite the criticism and difficulties with mainline denominations, the ASSU was a valuable evangelistic tool among the early settlers, preparing individuals for conversion. As the country expanded westward, the formation of a Sunday School often brought together children on the prairie. School houses were constructed, with the common school and the Sunday School sharing the same building in town after town. As the children were evangelized, their parents were affected, communities formed, and preachers sought to bring them into a church. The Sunday School was not a church but an institutional entrance into the local church. By the 1860s, the various denominations took over running Sunday Schools attached to their congregations. They began to produce their own lesson materials. Alongside common schools, which focused on basic education, Sunday Schools were now able to emphasize denominational teachings.

There were two church bodies that heretofore had not been part of the Sunday School phenomenon, the Lutherans and the Roman Catholics. The Lutheran Church—Missouri Synod began in this same period with the settlement of the Saxon Lutherans along the Mississippi River watershed while other German Lutherans settled throughout the Midwest. Lutheran doctrine, liturgical worship, strong ethnic background, and language barriers prohibited them from joining in the Sunday School movement. For many of the same reasons, the Roman Catholic Church was even more reluctant to join in the Sunday School movement. Part of the frustration lay in the nature of the Sunday School model. It did not center instruction in the worship of the congregation, or look to the pastor or priest as the chief teacher of the faith, nor did it include the home as a vital part of a child's religious instruction.

These concerns, while articulated by many mainline denominations, were felt greatly in the Lutheran community. For Lutherans, the congregation found its center and life in worship, in the worship service where God's Word is preached and His gifts are given. In Lutheran theology, the pastor, who stands in the stead and by the command of God, is the chief teacher and authority in regard to matters of faith. Likewise, home instruction of children was practiced as outlined in Scripture, by Luther and the Early Church Fathers.

Lutherans also saw that the common schools established throughout the country were strongly affected by Protestant doctrine. This fact, in addition to the very Protestant Sunday Schools, was enough to cause them to develop their own educational systems. Here was the initial impetus for the Lutheran parochial school system. Almost as soon as Lutheran congregations were formed, they established Christian Day Schools to teach their own children the cores subjects and Lutheran doctrine. They established colleges and seminaries to train their own teachers and pastors. But it was not until the early 1900s that Sunday Schools appeared in many Lutheran congregations.

In some respects, the development of the Sunday School in LCMS parishes was an acquiescing to the American religious culture. German Lutherans were an oddity on the American, English-speaking religious scene. Sunday School was viewed as a way to evangelize and draw people to church. Just as in the other denominations, early LCMS Sunday Schools were largely lay led and often self supporting.

In 1899, Concordia Publishing House began publishing materials for use in Lutheran Sunday Schools, along with home devotional and Bible storybooks. One hundred and seven years later, Sunday School is still an important and established part of Lutheran Church life. From the beginning, the Sunday Schools in our Synod have often been viewed as foster children, living alongside the naturally born day schools and confirmation classes. To some degree, the Sunday School is a self-contained program with little or no connection to the rest of the church, with some churches offering it as a children's alternative to the worship service.

It is helpful to understand the history and importance of Sunday School in both the Lutheran Church and on the American religious scene. Equally important is understanding what makes a Sunday School Lutheran, and why it is important to make such a distinction.

The Philosophy and Purpose of Sunday School

BY PAMELA NIELSEN

It's Sunday morning, and there you are with materials and supplies in hand as you scoot down the halls of your church, headed to your Sunday School classroom, eager to teach the children in your class. You and others the world over faithfully teach the Lord's little ones week after week, often in cramped or difficult settings, with few supplies and little support in this volunteer service.

Could I interrupt you for a moment to ask some questions? So why do you do it? What is the purpose of Sunday School? Who is it really for? And what constitutes a good Sunday School anyway? It's helpful to stop what we are doing once in a while to think through the reasons and purpose of our efforts—the *why*. Often such reflection aids in refocusing and fine-tuning our efforts so that they are truly worthwhile and fruitful. Such musing often gives us new perspectives and purpose. This chapter is designed to make you stop and think about the *why* of Sunday School. The rest of this volume is filled with ideas for events, working with special-needs children, selecting curriculum, using music, and a host of other practical and useful information.

Historically we know that Sunday School had its beginnings as a lay-led movement to help reign in neglected and needy children in the 1700s. And while today Sunday School is firmly entrenched in nearly every Protestant congregation worldwide, there is a lot of talk about the purpose of Sunday School, its structure, and its audience. Thoughts about these matters seem to vary widely. But as Lutherans, we are guided in all our efforts by our Confession of faith and understanding of God's Word. In many ways that makes us unique, but more importantly, it gives us a solid foundation for understanding why we do what we do. Sunday School is no exception.

Life-Giving Water

My home lies near the Mississippi River. Daily I encounter many of the rivers and tributaries that feed off of this ongoing source of life-supporting water. I think of the Church and her worship as being like a large, flowing river. This life-giving river flows out and sustains the lives of God's people through the Word clearly preached and through Holy Baptism and the Lord's Supper offered each Sunday. These feed God's people and nourish them for lives of thanks and praise, service and obedience in the Church and the world.

Every activity of the Church, including the Sunday School, resembles an off-shoot of a larger river. It may be another smaller river, a stream, or creek, but each has, and carries, the central source of life that came from the main river—life-giving water. In the Church, as God's people gather around Word and Sacrament, they are refreshed with forgiveness, life, and salvation poured out for them in the life, death, and resurrection of Jesus Christ.

Jesus told the woman of Samaria, "Whoever drinks of the water that I will give him will never be thirsty forever. The water that I will give him will become in him a spring of water welling up to eternal life" (John 4:14). So, too, in Sunday School, we pour out the water of life—Jesus Christ and His saving work for us. We teach that life comes from God who richly and daily provides all that we need. The Bible provides the message as students and teachers together explore the miraculous story of salvation which God worked in and through the lives of ordinary people like you and me.

From time to time—whether accidentally or intentionally—something other than water spills into the mighty Mississippi River. This pollutes the water, eventually harming all that draw their life from the river. Most vulnerable are the young plants and animals not strong enough to endure the intrusion of the foreign substance.

This is especially so in the Sunday School where the teaching of God's Word is directed toward children! How important it is that they get the pure Word of God, spoken clearly in a way that they can understand and drink in, not clouded by things that would distract or dilute God's Word.

In the world there is another river, one that flows in the opposite direction from the river of life. This river of sin and death seeks to destroy all in its path. The world places its focus on man and his work, efforts, and achievements. The message that life is about *our* individual wants and desires bombards you and your students in print, on television, and in the popular music of our day.

You, and the children you teach each week, are affected by this other river.

Your students in Sunday School are not immune to the effects of sin in their lives, the sin they have committed and the sin of others has affected them in many ways. God sent His Son as a cure for that sin.

In His perfect wisdom and grace, your heavenly Father called you to serve His little ones in Sunday School. This is a most blessed vocation! For many children this is the only time in their week when someone intentionally speaks God's saving Word to them and helps them to understand what it means. Let this guide you as you teach:

* *Teach the Word—God's Word! Sunday School exists to teach God's Word to children of all ages.*

* *Teach God's Law! Talk about sin, sin in the world, sin in your life, and the sin in your students' lives. Teach what God expects of us and make clear our desperate need for a Savior.*

* *Teach the Gospel! Every Sunday, make the message of Jesus Christ as Savior a central part of your teaching, letting it flow throughout the lesson. Point children to God's saving action for them in Christ Jesus at every opportunity.*

* *Focus on Christ as Savior! Often we become tempted to present Christ as a good example, or as a good friend. Certainly these are true things, but in terms of our eternal salvation from sin, death, and the devil, it is vital that you emphasize Christ as Savior each week. God sent His only Son to seek and save the lost.*

Targeting Your Audience

We say that Sunday School exists for children, but what kind of children? Some state that Sunday School is about outreach to children who don't know Jesus. Others argue that Sunday School should serve solely the congregation's children. I believe it needs to serve both. All children need to hear God's life-giving Word. Like you and me, children who are not connected to the river of life, live lives parched by sin. That is true for the baptized children in your congregation as well as the unknown children in your neighborhood. Let your Sunday School open its doors to any and all children in your church *and* community!

Is your Sunday School large, bustling with many children, or is it rather small with merely a few boys and girls? No matter! Each child is of worth to Jesus and thus is worth your time and effort to teach. The world tells us that numbers matter. The bigger the better! Our heavenly Father is concerned for each individual, numbering the very hairs on each head. It can be discouraging to teach a class of one or two while we long for a larger group, but God has led the children to your classroom, the many or the few. And each class size offers its own unique blessings and challenges.

There are many different approaches to Sunday School. In the pages of this book you will hear about some of them and you will read ideas for attracting students and keeping them coming to Sunday School. You will surely want to try some of these helpful ideas.

However, a word of caution is in order. In a world focused on entertainment and consumer satisfaction, the Church is often tempted to employ strategies and techniques designed to please and entertain in an effort to draw larger numbers. Certainly, there is no one way to do Sunday School but when our efforts to increase attendance involve watering down the message of God's Word or distracting from the Word with activities and games, then we have missed the point. If we are afraid to talk about sin because it might offend or upset someone, then there is a problem. If our goal is purely large numbers of happy, smiling children busy doing things, then our focus has shifted off of Christ.

Routine

God gives us all things for our use and depending on the ages of the children you teach you will employ different methods and strategies for teaching God's Word in order that they hear and understand the Word of Life. While adults often long for variety, young children especially need the comfort of routine. A strong Sunday School program will build in both variety and routine. What sort of things should be routine in a Lutheran Sunday School?

* *God's Word, read and taught from the Bible, should be at the center of every Sunday School lesson.*

* *Prayer—each week the lesson should open and close with prayer.*

* *Worship—model and connect the lesson to the Church's life of worship.*

* *Speak to your students, using the language of the faith.*

* *Speak of Jesus Christ as their Savior from sin, death, and the devil.*

God's Word

As part of your lesson you may elect to use puppets, a skit, a Bible storybook, and other approaches to telling the story. These approaches help capture the children's attention and draw them into the lesson. Even so, it is vital that each week you also let the children know that what they are learning comes from the Bible—God's Word. Have a Bible handy and read all or parts of the story from it for that week. With older children have Bibles for the readers in your class and let them read from God's Word, even if only a few verses. Lesson leaflets are temporary, and are often discarded after the lesson concludes, but your students will come to know the Bible week after week.

When we read from the Bible we communicate a message of importance and permanence to the words that are read. God's Word comes with God's promise: "So shall My word be that goes out from My mouth; it shall not return to Me empty, but it shall accomplish that which I purpose, and shall succeed in the thing for which I sent it" (Isaiah 55:11).

These words from God take the burden off of you as teacher—God will work through His Word. You present that Word and trust your heavenly Father to work in the hearts and lives of the children you teach. Knowing this, you are free to enjoy teaching rather than fret about it. When your lesson is firmly rooted in God's Word, you can teach boldly.

Prayer

Jesus taught His disciples to pray. Scripture is filled with prayer and invitations to pray. Open and close your Sunday School with prayer. In so doing you teach by example how to pray, as well as the value and importance of prayer. Allow children to participate or lead the prayers from time to time. Sunday School is a place to learn about the things of God and His Church. Let the students learn by doing.

While extemporaneous prayers are fine for those who are comfortable with praying on-the-spot, it is helpful if you introduce several prayers that children can learn and use all through their lives. The Lord's Prayer is certainly the most well-known memorized prayer. Martin Luther's Morning and Evening Prayers are also wonderful prayers to commit to memory. If you have a snack time in Sunday School, this provides a wonderful time to teach some simple meal prayers.

Worship

The church's life begins and flows from the gathering of God's people to receive the gifts of Word, water, and bread and wine in the worship service. Children from a very young age discern that something important and unique is happening in the church service. Sunday School provides a perfect opportunity to teach children about the church's worship in small doses, with intentional teaching as you relate worship to the Bible lessons you teach.

As a large group or a single class, consider setting up a small altar with a white cloth, two candles, a cross, and a Bible. Use this space to gather around when you open and close your Sunday School. Enlist the children to set up the altar, read the Scriptures, light the candles, collect the offering, and so forth. Teach about appropriate behavior in church. Talk about the Church Year and its colors and themes. Introduce the Church's song—her hymns and liturgy to the children. Deliberately teaching these elements enables children to participate in your church's worship.

Speak

As Lutherans we speak about our faith in Christ Jesus in a distinctive way. The words we use come from the Bible and our Lutheran Confessions, most specifically from the Small Catechism and the hymnal. Let these treasures guide your speaking about the faith in Sunday School. For all people, but especially children, hearing and learning become most effective when the same words are employed over and over again. Repetition is an important teacher. Once one understands the words, they are free to really explore what those words mean. If the words change frequently it leads to confusion and uncertainty.

How beautiful it is when a child hears a Bible verse or learns a phrase from the catechism or liturgy and then hears it spoken in church by all of God's people! This is a connecting point for the child, communicating that what goes on in the church is for him or her. Young children are thrilled when they can sing a hymn or say the creed or part of the liturgy with everyone else in church. Sunday School provides an important opportunity for making this connection with children!

Christ as Savior

Regardless of whether your lesson is from the Old or New Testament, no matter the topic, it must always point to Christ Jesus as Savior and Redeemer from sin and death. Be careful to avoid only speaking of Jesus as a moral leader, a good example to follow. That way of speaking turns the Gospel of the Lord into the Law for us, demanding that we live up to the standard He set for us. We can never live as perfectly as Jesus, thus we confess our total dependence on Christ and His work, and teach our children that the key to our salvation is faith in Christ Jesus as our Savior.

Other Routines

Other routines are important as well. The structure of your class, how you arrange your room, and the order of the lesson are especially important to the very young, who equate routine with security. Children also need structure for the opening and closing celebrations. Be sure to celebrate birthdays and Baptism birthdays, establishing a routine for honoring these special milestones.

Variety

What about variety in the Sunday School? There are many opportunities for variety each week as you teach Sunday School. This book is filled with a host of ideas that will add variety. In the Sunday School there are several places where variety is often a welcome component—in your lesson materials, in the presentation of the Bible story, in the location where your class meets, and in the organization of the whole Sunday School in your congregation.

Lesson Materials

The curriculum you use for your Sunday School will likely suggest a variety of activities and approaches to teaching the Bible story. You are the expert in your class, use what works and skip the ideas that don't. If the children in your class really enjoy a certain activity or teaching method, don't be afraid to use it more than once, adapting other lessons to incorporate these favorite teaching strategies, which may well become part of your routine!

Understanding the purpose of Sunday School, with its central message of Jesus

Christ and the salvation He won for us on the cross, will guide your teaching and your choice of techniques and activities that you use in your class. Lesson plans from a Sunday School publisher are merely guides offering choices for teaching. A good lesson plan is designed to offer flexibility so it can be effective in many situations and settings. Some suggestions will not work in your setting—others will be the perfect idea—you choose!

Children enjoy planned and purposeful variety. Think through the options you have and consider your students and their abilities and preferences. Make sure the choices you make are done in an effort to aid the clear communicating of God's Word to the children. Variety for variety's sake often brings frustration. Variety for entertainment's sake has the wrong goal. Variety with the purpose of strengthening the teaching of God's Word is a benefit to the students, helping them to learn the lesson you have taught well.

Presenting the Bible Story

Though it is imperative to read all or part of the story from the Bible each week, you will also want to introduce or review the story with a variety of techniques. Dramatic readings, acting out the story with actors or puppets, using chalk or markers to draw the story, using hymns to tell the story, classic art images of various Bible stories, Bible storybooks, skits, and guest storytellers all are wonderful ways to reinforce the Bible story. Your lesson materials will offer some options for unique ways to present the story, and there are many resource books available with creative ideas for you to try.

Location, Location, Location

Consider moving your class once in a while to a new setting for the lesson. Perhaps it is a sunny day and your lesson is about Jesus feeding or teaching the multitudes. You might consider taking a blanket outside and sitting on the grass with your students as you tell the Bible story. Or if the lesson is about worship or the elements of worship, consider taking the students to the sanctuary and have the lesson in the front of the church or around the baptismal font. Have you considered field trips? If your lesson is on the Last Supper, plan ahead to meet the pastor or the head of the Altar Guild in the sacristy. Have them show the students how the Communionware is stored and prepared for use. Ask your pastor if he would allow the students into his vestry where he could display and explain his vestments and the matching altar paraments.

Organization

How you organize your Sunday School program is yet another choice. Many churches employ the traditional one class and one teacher per grade level. Others do what is known as Large Group/Small Group Sunday School, still others have found the Site Rotation or Rotation model works best for them. How you structure your

Sunday School classes will be dependent on the number and ages of the students and the number of volunteer teachers and helpers that are available. There is a chapter on Sunday School models in this book which will help you explore the possibilities for your program.

Activities, music, crafts, and special events are all ways to offer helpful variety that will aid in teaching God's Word to the children in your Sunday School. Explore the pages of this handy volume and consider the many possibilities! May the Lord bless your efforts with His little ones!

staffing

Staffing Your Sunday School

BY LOU JANDER

Just a few days ago I got a note from a pastor asking me that almost famous question, "Do you have any ideas for recruiting and keeping Sunday School teachers?" He went on to say, "I know you don't have a 'magic solution' but we have to do something to stop the bleeding and get back to having teachers for all of our classes. Our attendance has also been declining."

I was looking for a book on the bookshelves the other day and ran across a book titled *Solving Church Education's Ten Toughest Problems* by John R. Cionca, written in 1990. Now that's a good number of years ago, but right off the bat he deals with the issue of recruiting staff. Here's his list of the ten toughest problems facing church education:

* *Recruiting of staff*

* *Poor follow-up of pupils by teachers*

* *Teacher training*

* *Teacher burnout and turnover*

* *Lack of Bible memorization*

* *Apathy and declining attendance*

* *Coordination of the Christian education program*

* Lack of use of the church library

* Resistance to change

* Developing a home Bible study ministry

Interesting isn't it! It seems that these same issues, with slight modifications, remain with us today and have been with us for some time. So what do we do about it? Maybe it's time to step up and take some action! Maybe it's time to be bold in dealing with the reality of declining Sunday Schools and recognize the contributing factors.

Much of what is being written today regarding building a Sunday School program or recruiting workers centers on identifying the significance of the Sunday School and the important role that it plays in our Christian training and discipleship. There was a time when the Sunday School was a well-accepted and highly respected agency of Christian education. A time back then when people committed two to three hours on Sunday morning to worship and Sunday School. Now it's hard to get people to commit one hour to anything at church on Sunday morning. Be assured, finding Sunday School teachers isn't the only "recruiting" issue in congregations these days. I hear the same concerns about finding people to serve on boards and committees. Finding motivated, passionate, willing workers these days is no walk in the park.

I would like to submit that finding staff for the Sunday School or for other areas of ministry in the congregation starts with values. What is important to me—what I believe is worth spending my time doing—will get my time!

People measure things today based on time. Time is the currency of the day! Whatever happened to all the "leisure" time that was suppose to be available; the 30-hour workweek; the extra time that we would have because of computers; the many timesaving devices that have come into our homes and on and on. Research continues to indicate that people are pressed by time. There are so many places to go and things to do, that choices have to be made. We systematically seek to prioritize our time!

Defining Priorities

Even in this day and age of time-sensitive choices, I make choices based on what is important to me. Let me illustrate just how important values are in making decisions. Some of the readers of this book may be acquainted with Bluebell Ice Cream. It's made in Texas, and the little creamery in Brenham, Texas, is a favorite place to visit. It boasts of having the best homemade vanilla, off the shelf, ice cream around (I, of course, would agree). I've tried others—just about all of them—and truly there is no other homemade vanilla that compares. Are you getting the sense that I value Bluebell? When I go to a restaurant the wait staff invariably asks at the end of the meal whether I would like some dessert. I always ask if they have ice cream. Almost always, the answer is, yes. Then I pop the BIG question, What brand is it? If they don't know, I ask them to find out. When they return and give the answer as something other than Bluebell, I decline dessert. That's just how much I value having what I believe to be the very best. I'll literally pass up a dessert simply because the ice cream isn't the right brand. I know that's a stretch—but we make choices based on what we value—based on what we have come to believe and expect.

So how does this relate to staffing Sunday School? If Sunday School is important to me and important in the life and ministry of the congregation, when asked to participate, I am more likely to respond with a favorable "Yes, I would like to be involved." The more I believe in Sunday School the more likely I will give my time and energy to serving as needed.

The way a person feels about Sunday School may very well reflect the priority placed on it by the church. Just how important is Christian education? What amount of time and resources are allocated to the various areas of Christian education?

In 1990, Search Institute completed a comprehensive study of six mainline denominations regarding faith development and faith maturity. That study was adapted, expanded, and conducted in The Lutheran Church—Missouri Synod in 1993. The report, *Congregations at the Crossroads*, was then shared with the leadership of the Church. The two studies concluded that Christian education plays a vital part in the continued faith development of children.

The study also identified other helpful information regarding the relationship between interactive learning, having an integrated faith, and loyalty to the ministry of the congregation. An integrated faith is one where the individual's faith impacts other areas of their life. Their thinking, behavior, and daily living are "colored" by their faith.

So, the bottom line is that the Church needs to lift up the importance of Sunday School and the significant contribution that it makes in the faith life and development of children, youth, and adults. The greater the recognition of Sunday School in the life and ministry of the congregation, the greater the possibility of people wanting to be part of the teaching staff. Thus, recruitment gets easier! If a church as a whole recognized the importance of Sunday School, it would help individuals view Sunday School as important.

Here are just a few ways that a church might build up the importance of its Sunday School:

1. *Build a culture that begins to see worship and Bible study as one event on Sunday morning—where Bible study flows out of the worship life of the congregation.*

2. *Speak of Sunday School as part of the commitment that new members make when joining the congregation.*

3. *Involve the Sunday School in the worship services.*

4. *Don't send children out of worship—help them feel a part of the family of God.*

5. *Don't plan worship during the time of Sunday School. This only creates the opportunity for parents to send children to Sunday School while they attend worship, thus creating values in children and adults for the future.*

6. *Recognize the Sunday School and the teachers in different activities and events in the congregation.*

7. *Allot adequate financial resources for Sunday School.*

8. *See the mission possibilities of the Sunday School.*

9. *Talk about it, tell about it, preach about it, publicize it, make it extremely visible.*

10. *Make it easy for visitors to get their children and themselves into Sunday School.*

11. *Make a big event of the time when children start Sunday School.*

12. *See Sunday School as all-inclusive, not just for kids—but people of all ages.*

Creating a Problem

Moving on to yet another issue in staffing the Sunday School, I'm reminded of something my dad used to say to folks who didn't buy the tools that he was selling, "You get what you pay for." Sound familiar? Well, I believe that staffing has become a problem in most churches because we've made it a problem.

I remember sitting in an adjoining office one evening at a congregation I was serving and listening to the Sunday School superintendent making phone calls trying to find a couple of teachers. While I could only hear one side of the conversations that he had, I could just imagine what was going through the mind of the person on the other side. "I'm calling to see if you would be able to teach grade 4 in our Sunday School. . . . Oh, it won't take much time and you don't have to do much preparation. . . . Yes, I understand how difficult it might be to attend the meetings, but, well, don't worry about that. . . . Oh, we can get a substitute if you have to miss a Sunday. . . . Well, if you could just be there 50 percent of the time that would be great. . . . Well, maybe next time we need someone, I'll call and see if you would be interested then." End of phone call.

Now why in the world would anyone want to teach in that Sunday School? Low expectations, low motivation, no need for training, and on and on . . . got the picture? "Don't ask me to do something that seems such a waste of time and that doesn't seem important."

If you want to have sufficient volunteers to staff the Sunday School, you will need to remember two key points: (1) retention means fewer replacements; (2) recruit and train before the need arises.

Retention

In order to retain teachers we must recognize, support, and train teachers. Recognizing teachers isn't rocket science. It's simply acknowledging the important role that they are performing. That acknowledging comes from positive words of encouragement, one-on-one. Acknowledging teachers comes through recognizing them as key servants in the life of the congregation. Appreciation may be demonstrated further through personal notes, words of affirmation from the pastor, from the director of Christian education, from the superintendent, and from key leaders in the congregation.

Retention is also accomplished by providing ongoing support. Support comes in many forms. Teachers are supported with

* attractively decorated and educationally designed classrooms;

* teaching materials that provide resources for the teaching/learning
    process;

* continuous opportunities to enrich teaching skills;

* an agreed upon term of service; and

* visits from the pastor in the classroom.

Do all that you can to recognize the important work of the Sunday School teacher. Find new ways to offer support and make that a habit.

Teacher Training

It's interesting to note that there are many roles or jobs that cannot be done without training; in fact, many positions require prior training. Take for example an officer in the air force. Before you can fly a plane, you have to be trained. Before being promoted to squadron commander, you must go through training. The promotion to wing commander means successful work as a squadron commander, followed by training to be a wing commander. You don't move through the various ranks without some type of training.

Training Sunday School teachers starts before there is a need. We know we're going to have to have some replacements. So why not begin the training process so that those in training can observe trained teachers in action. After all, most people learn best by observing others and by practicing.

Before a person enters full-time teaching in an educational institution, training is required. Training begins as a student with classroom work in the theories and methodologies of teaching. Then comes "student teaching" with a certified teacher, and finally, the process of certification.

If teaching Sunday School is considered important, then we ought to be equipping teachers for the significant work they will be doing. Here are six areas that might be covered in preparing Sunday School teachers:

1. *Teacher Training. Teaching is a craft that constantly requires sharpening one's skills as a communicator. The better the teaching, the more likely the resulting growth.*

2. *Leadership Skills. This includes categories such as planning, scheduling, determining and setting goals for teaching, and understanding various age-level learning needs and competencies.*

3. *People Skills. Teaching is all about people. We need to learn to work with them effectively.*

4. *Spiritual Development. It is important that teachers keep growing in their own spiritual journey. Training should provide skills for continued personal growth.*

5. *Biblical Content. Old Testament Survey, New Testament Survey, Doctrine, and similar studies should strengthen the lives of our teachers and the material they will be teaching.*

6. *Evangelism. This area is important as we see the Sunday School as an outreach arm of the church.*

If we want to strengthen our staffing in Sunday School and desire a quality Sunday School program, we must commit to providing ongoing and frequent training opportunities. We need to develop clear expectations for our teachers to be involved in that training. Inviting those who might consider teaching to training events may help provide them with a better understanding and appreciation of the important work Sunday School involves. When perspective teachers meet jointly with the experienced teachers, they can learn from one another and develop relationships of mutual support in the process—in short, becoming a team.

Methods of Recruitment

We have talked about the importance of lifting up Sunday School as a significant part of the church's ministry. That's one side of recruitment. The other side of properly staffing our Sunday Schools has to do with some key things to remember when securing new staff.

First, let me suggest a bit of a change here. Throughout this chapter I've used the term *recruit* or *recruitment*. Let me suggest that we consider a different word, *enlistment*. *Enlist* or *enlistment* more readily describes what we are attempting to do. The word *enlist* is defined as "to secure the support and aid of; employ in advancing an interest; or to participate heartily." *Staffing* may be a good word to use in identifying this chapter, but what we are really talking about is enlisting people for service in God's kingdom. *Recruiting* sounds like work; *enlisting* gives the impression of securing people to participate in an exciting venture called Sunday School.

Now let's talk about some things to remember when enlisting people for service in Sunday School:

Identify potential individuals who might serve by asking others, or by looking through the church directory. If your congregation gathers talent records or gift inventories look at these tools for potential teachers.

Talk to these individuals personally; that means in person. The phone has more and more become an instrument for soliciting products and simply conveying information. If what we are asking individuals to consider is important, than it behooves us to talk to them face-to-face. And that isn't always best done following a worship service or when we "catch them at church." Instead, make an appointment to visit them in their home. Take along some good resource material like the lesson material for the grade you will be asking the individual to teach or a brochure highlighting the purpose of Sunday School in your congregation.

Provide the candidate with a position description (a sample is provided at the end of this chapter) and review that with the candidate. Don't forget to include the expectations of the teacher as well as what the teacher can expect from the congregation.

* *Identify how the church supports the teacher in the important role of Sunday School teacher.*

* *Don't minimize the preparation time or the training plan. This is important work and thus takes a commitment to the process.*

* *Be clear on the time frame that you are requesting the individual to consider. This isn't a "lifelong commitment" but one that has a clear starting point and ending point.*

* *While it doesn't produce grand results, it still is a good idea to "advertise" the staffing needs for the next Sunday School year. But remember, this isn't something that is done only once a year. Enlisting Sunday School teachers is an ongoing process that is always "in process." Bring prospective teachers into your training program year round.*

* *Encourage candidates to talk with existing teachers about their experience. It isn't a bad idea to have lined this up with individuals who are currently teaching. Let current teachers know that someone may contact them so they can be prepared.*

* *Pray before visiting with a candidate. Let the candidate know that you will be praying for him or her as he or she considers the request that you are making.*

* *Send the candidate a note of thanks immediately after your visit. Use this opportunity to again provide encouragement as the candidate considers the request to teach in your Sunday School.*

* *When a candidate notifies you that he or she will be able to teach, say "thanks," but also send a personal letter of thanks. If you are doing long-term enlisting, this is the time to invite the candidate to attend a training class. That class should be a thorough introduction to the*

*teaching role. If the candidate notifies you that he or she will not be able
to teach at this time, send a note of thanks anyway.*

It's Your Turn

So, there are some thoughts about staffing the Sunday School. God provides us with the resources to carry out His ministry. Just remember these key points as you go about staffing your Sunday School:

* *Sunday Schools that are valued are worth spending time with.*

* *Good retention builds for the future.*

* *Training creates excitement, raises the level of competency, and lifts the level of importance.*

* *Use important and personal methods for staffing.*

* *Consider the word enlistment instead of recruitment.*

Sunday School Teacher

Preschool through Sixth Grade

Definition:

A Sunday School teacher works with a specific group of students as a guide, caregiver, instructor, mentor, and leader as the group proceeds through growth in and study of God's Word.

The teacher will

* pray regularly for their students;

* prepare to teach;

* grow in teaching skills;

* care for the students and their families;

* commit to a specific length of time for teaching;

* contact visitors to the class;

* follow up on absent students;

* be an example in the study of Scripture and personal devotion;

* share his or her faith with students, families, and others;

* actively seek out new students.

The church will

* pray regularly for the teacher;

* provide materials that are sound doctrinally and educationally;

* offer teacher training opportunities;

* minister to the teacher in all circumstances;

* commit to honoring teaching timetables;

* recognize, support, and affirm the work of the teacher;

* constantly lift up the Sunday School as an important part of Christian education and the church's ministry.

Qualifications:

1. *Must have a love for children.*

2. *Must be a church member and regularly attend worship services.*

3. *Must have an interest and desire to communicate God's Word.*

4. *No teaching experience required. Training provided.*

Staff Development

BY DAVID G. EBELING

Sunday School is a mission of the congregation traditionally placed in the hands of volunteers to organize and teach the classes. Typically, one individual is identified as the Sunday School superintendent while others are asked to teach. A lay board usually oversees the program. Sunday School normally runs on its own, until the superintendent quits or, more crucially, a faithful teacher resigns or moves away.

Staff development includes those things the congregational leaders, especially the pastor, Sunday School superintendent, and Board of Christian Education, do to encourage and assist the Sunday School teachers in carrying out their ministry to and with children. An important component of staff development for Sunday School teachers is for the congregation to offer at least a quarterly staff training session led by the pastor or his designee. It's better yet if this is a monthly session of at least an hour.

Staff development starts by identifying potential candidates and inviting the best people available to teach. Once they are on the staff, training those who teach and encouraging them in their service are critical factors for having an effective Sunday School in your congregation.

Staff development, when neglected, can lead to teacher frustration, isolation in the classroom, and dissatisfaction. Ignoring staff development will likely result in short-term, burned-out teachers; and congregational leaders constantly scrambling to

25

find new members to teach, instead of using energy and resources to support and encourage those who are already doing the teaching.

Staff development often takes place when the teachers meet together under the direction of the pastor, the Sunday School superintendent, a director of Christian education, or another designated, skilled leader. (In this chapter, *staff development* and *teachers meetings* are used interchangeably.)

This chapter addresses three topics related to staff development for Sunday School teachers:

1. *Four tasks to identify Sunday School teacher candidates who will also participate in staff development.*

2. *Ten components of teachers meetings for Sunday School teachers.*

3. *Teacher Recognition as a critical element of staff development.*

Identifying Adults to Teach Sunday School

Your opportunity to have a successful and effective Sunday School will likely be based on the quality of the teacher(s) in the classroom(s). In an arena of limited volunteers, identifying the candidates most likely to succeed is your first goal. Don't wait for the best-qualified candidates to come to you. Do your homework. Look for people who might not even consider volunteering, but may welcome the opportunity to become a Sunday School teacher when approached with a specific purpose in mind. As you identify potential volunteers, keep in mind that they need to be open to continued growth as a Christian educator.

Task #1: Finding Candidates Who Might Be Teachers

Consider any candidate who responds to a notice ("Sunday School Teacher Needed") in your church bulletin or newsletter. Better yet, seek and invite candidates in a systematic way. For each of the statements listed below, write the name of at least one person who fits that description. This is simply a personal brainstorming exercise to begin a list of potential teachers. If you can do this exercise with another church member who knows the congregation well, or the pastor, and/or the Board of Education, the list is likely to be more complete. Remember, when possible, write down at least one name, preferably two or three names, for each descriptive statement, even if you've never considered them in a teaching role before.

Write at least one name of . . .

* *moms or dads of children who have good attendance in Sunday School.*

* *grandfathers and/or grandmothers of children in your congregation.*

* *professional educators who teach in public or Christian schools or universities.*

* *adults with teaching credentials or experience who no longer work in that field.*

* those who have previously taught Sunday School, but are not currently teaching.

* college students on a career track related to teaching.

* newer members who have yet to be invited to be involved in this aspect of congregational life.

* people who attend church virtually every Sunday.

* members who participate in at least one weekly Bible study sponsored by your congregation.

* adults who carry their personal Bible in church and for Bible classes.

Look for names that were listed under two or more descriptors. You especially want people who were identified in one of the last three descriptors, those who have a passion for studying God's Word. Not only is this an important teaching criteria, it also helps point to potential teachers who will continue to value Bible study as a part of their role as a Sunday School teacher.

Task #2: Deciding Characteristics and Qualifications

Teaching children and youth is an awesome task. Before going any further, pause in prayer, asking our heavenly Father to give you wisdom in identifying those who might teach and want to continue to learn themselves. Pray also for God to open the hearts of those invited to accept the role of teacher.

Prepare a position description. Use this template (or the example on pp. 34–35) as the framework for creating a position description unique to your congregation and the class you need to fill. Notice that the last two items are in reference to ongoing staff development. The point is that you state up front, as part of the invitation and position description, that participating in staff development and teacher meetings is expected. The first step is for the Board to decide the parameters of experience and responsibility for candidates. These might include:

1. *Sunday School teacher candidates have been active members of the congregation for a full year before being assigned a class; show evidence of a desire to study God's Word personally.*

2. *Two teachers are assigned to each class, so that at least one of them can be present each Sunday, with both teachers present whenever possible.*

3. *Potential teachers with little experience are assigned to serve as an observer or aide before being assigned her or his own class.*

4. *The congregation purchases all the teacher and student materials for the teachers' use.*

5. *Teachers value building personal relationships with the children and take time to do so regularly.*

6. *Generally, the Sunday School teacher can expect to commit about ten*

hours per month to this role: an hour each week to prepare, plus an hour each Sunday to teach, plus time spent in prayer, planning, and learning with other Sunday School teachers.

7. *The teachers regularly participate in the monthly teachers meeting to increase their biblical knowledge and teaching skills. (This is staff development!)*

Task #3: Writing a Sunday School Teacher Position Description

Use the statements below (and on pp. 34–35) as a template to create a position description that outlines the expectations that your congregation has of its teachers. Reproducible examples are on pages 34 and 35.

Sunday School *Teacher of the Faith* Position Description.

Teachers of the Faith are important servants of Christ in our congregation because they have direct contact and influence with children, their parents, and other members of our congregation. The statements below will provide you with a sense of the task you are undertaking.

Teachers of the faith . . .

* *serve for a period of one year, eligible for annual renewal.*

* *are to consider prayerfully every lesson as it is prepared to be taught.*

* *regard highly the spiritual needs of the children and their families entrusted to their care.*

* *strive to teach in ways that will promote the spiritual growth, health, and nurture of the children in the class.*

* *make the classroom space attractive and inviting for the learners.*

* *pray continually for their learners and for blessing upon the Sunday School programs.*

* *faithfully attend all training sessions and staff meetings offered for their benefit.*

* *arrive in their classrooms ten to fifteen minutes before the children arrive to be sure all is ready and to be able to focus on the individual children as they arrive.*

* *care for children and their families who are irregular in attendance, in cooperation with the pastor, elders, and Sunday School superintendent.*

* *supervise their students in any activities in which the students participate, such as singing in a worship service.*

* *become friends and counselors to their students. When possible, visit the homes of the students to use every means to establish rapport with the children and their families.*

In recognition of the important role of Sunday School teachers in our congregation, we, the leaders of this congregation, pledge to . . .

* appoint teachers to their positions on the recommendation of the Sunday School superintendent or the Board of Christian Education with approval of our pastor and the elders.

* pray for the teachers in worship, staff meetings, and personal prayers.

* provide Christ-centered curriculum and related support materials in sufficient numbers for the students in the class.

* provide a budget line for teachers to secure additional teaching tools and related supplies for their classrooms.

* conduct regular teacher meetings that are timely, useful, and lead to a more effective Sunday School program.

* regularly feature information and articles about the Sunday School in the church bulletin, newsletters, and Web site.

Task #4: Writing and Sending a Letter of Invitation to Teaching Candidate(s)

Now you are ready to extend the invitation. While this certainly can be done in an informal, verbal way, consider sending a personal letter of invitation. It may read something like this sample but adapt the letter to fit your specific needs. Send the invitation to teach on church stationery.

Dear Janet,

This letter comes with an invitation for you to consider. I am praying that you'll read through this letter and that the Holy Spirit will move you to ponder the possibilities it offers.

Last Sunday, when the Sunday School children sang in church, I noticed the intent look and loving, caring smile on your face that reflected through your eyes. It appears that you really enjoy children and also deeply love Jesus, our Savior.

We are planning for next fall and are looking for a few selected individuals to help with our church's Sunday School program. Christian education is very important in our congregation. Our goal is to touch the lives of all children from birth through grade 6 by sharing the Good News of Jesus with them in as many ways as possible. We also try to equip parents to nurture their children in their homes.

At our church, we offer Sunday School, Vacation Bible School, and a weekday Christian kid's club. I am asking you to consider working in the Sunday School portion of this effort. You have been carefully and prayerfully nominated, with the approval of the pastor and the Boards of Elders and Education.

I will follow up with a personal phone call to you to explain what role you might play and the expectations for Sunday School staff members. In the meantime, please read over the enclosed position description. Please pray with me that God would lead you to a comfortable decision of service to Him.

In Christ,

[Superintendent or Pastor or Chair of the Board of Education (or all three)]

Ten Components of Staff Development for Sunday School Teachers

When you finally gather together for teachers meetings, begin on time, have an agenda, and use the time effectively. Here are ten components that could be included on your agenda. Seldom would you do all ten in the same meeting, but you should consider all of these issues over a period of a year.

1. Preview the lessons

Open up the curriculum materials for the coming weeks—between this meeting and the next. The pastor or his designee should spend a proportionate amount of time on each lesson. Give background information, set the lesson story in its biblical context, and identify the main ideas that must be emphasized. Allow time for questions and answers. Have teachers bring along and use their personal Bibles.

2. Focus on doctrine and beliefs

As Lutherans who belong to a Confessional Church, we say out loud what we believe, based on the Word of God. Consider using some of the teacher meeting time for a review of the Six Chief Parts of Luther's Small Catechism. Point out specific doctrines and beliefs and how a reference to them can and should be integrated into the Sunday School lesson.

3. Review an article about teaching or Sunday School

Order multiple copies of *Teachers Interaction*, a quarterly magazine for Christian Sunday School teachers. In advance of the teachers meeting, give each teacher a current copy. Assign one or more teachers the responsibility to read an article in advance of the meeting and give a summary and/or review of it to the rest of the staff. Discuss the reviewer's observations and underline several key statements in the article. This technique helps provide a focus for group discussion.

4. Get specific about teaching techniques

Take time to give concrete ideas about managing a classroom and dealing with disciplining of students in their care. Talk about topics like (1) making an attractive classroom setting, (2) interacting with children before class begins, (3) pacing the lesson, and (4) drawing the lesson to a close in the last few minutes. Consider inviting a local educator to plan and lead this component. (See chapter 7, The Sunday School Classroom, for more ideas.)

5. View and discuss teacher-training videos

Quite a few Christian publishers offer video-based training materials. In these, a skilled educator models and explains various techniques for the volunteer teacher. The kits usually include a viewers' guide with study questions and additional information for the leader. Often they are organized in brief segments so they can be used over a period of time.

6. Discuss specific student needs

Sunday School students cover the full range of learning skills, biblical knowledge, and maturity. It is appropriate in teachers meetings to discuss issues that come up in the Sunday School classroom. Others in the group may deal with similar circumstances, have siblings of a particular student, or offer suggestions of ways they have handled incidents in the past. Such discussion brings out additional ideas of ways to have an effective classroom.

7. Plan ways for the Sunday School to be visible to the congregation

Visibility is any way in which the work that learners produce in a Sunday School classroom is visible to someone not involved in Sunday School. Consider maintaining a bulletin board that features student work or photos of the staff. Schedule your Sunday School children to sing any of their Sunday School songs as a part of a worship service. Have a class prepare a brief dramatization of a Bible story and then arrange for a "performance" at a church social event or an adult Bible class.

8. Pray for the congregation, the children, the families, yourselves

Designate part of each teachers meeting for prayer. Ask each teacher to pray out loud for one particular student and family. Pray for wisdom, skill, and patience for the teaching staff. Consider the possibility of having prayer partners, a person *not* involved in Sunday School, but one willing to receive a list of teachers and students so that person can regularly pray for one particular class. That prayer partner could also contact the teacher each week with words of encouragement and ask for specific prayer requests.

9. Celebrate faith development milestones in your children's learning

Invite your teachers to tell their stories—stories about a particularly insightful response that a student made to a question, stories of students and their families who are experiencing particularly difficult times, stories about love and care expressed by one student to another, or stories about how a student threw a curve into the lesson and it turned out even better than expected. Every teacher has stories. Invite them to tell those stories.

10. Community building

Your Sunday School runs more smoothly, has more staff cohesiveness, and teachers meetings are much better attended when those who attend enjoy being together. Occasionally go around the table with an invitation for each teacher to respond in one or two minutes to starter statements such as (1) Introduce us to one or your childhood teachers who is still a model for you; or (2) Describe a setting in the recent past in which something you taught the children became important in your personal life; or (3) Tell where you fit in the birth order in your family and name one

staff development

student you know who is in the same position in his or her family. Create your own starter statements.

Teacher Recognition as a Critical Element of Staff Development

Sunday School teachers seldom choose this volunteer position so they can get recognized. They are typically humble, committed Christians who serve in response to the love of Jesus and their desire to tell the Good News of the Gospel of Jesus Christ. Many of them shun publicity or personal applause. Yet, the congregation does well to recognize their work and their ministry. Here are several ways to recognize teachers for you to consider:

* *Install teachers each year, probably in late summer, in a regular worship service. Ask teachers to publicly declare their readiness and willingness to teach God's Word to children and, likewise, ask the congregation to support their efforts.*

* *List the teachers in your monthly newsletter as volunteer teaching staff members.*

* *Provide identification for the teacher: a name tag to be worn every Sunday, the teacher's name on a door or wall near the teaching space. Produce a directory of teacher names including their classroom locations and grade taught that is distributed to all families.*

* *Annually present a teaching tool to each teacher to be kept as a personal item, even after the teacher retires from teaching. This might be a book about teaching, a reference book such as a Bible concordance, a DVD with maps and background information on biblical customs, or any other item that will enhance the teachers' personal and classroom knowledge.*

* *Put a surprise note in the teachers' congregational mailbox expressing appreciation for the services they are providing.*

* *Plan an annual recognition dinner, perhaps served by others in the congregation. In lieu of the last teachers meeting of the year, host a dinner at a local restaurant. Invite the teachers' spouses as well.*

* *Recruit one parent or grandparent from each class to send a note of appreciation to their child's or grandchild's teacher.*

It Makes Good Sense . . .

Managers in the business world know that it is just as important to keep an existing customer, as it is to get a new one—it's also easier to retain costumers than it is to drum up new ones. As a result, good managers do all they can to keep their current customers satisfied and content. In congregational life, it's equally important to keep your Sunday School teachers informed, trained, content, and appreciated. Doing so through staff development or well-organized and useful teachers meetings keeps Sunday School teachers on your volunteer list.

3

33

basics

Sample Sunday School Teacher Position Description

Teacher Qualifications

1. Sunday School teacher candidates have been active members of the congregation for a full year before being assigned a class; show evidence of a desire to study God's Word personally.

2. Two teachers are assigned to each class, so that at least one of them can be present each Sunday, with both teachers present whenever possible.

3. Potential teachers with little experience are assigned to serve as an observer or aide before being assigned his or her own class.

4. The congregation purchases all the teacher and student materials for the teachers' use.

5. Teachers value building personal relationships with the children and take time to do so regularly.

6. Generally, the Sunday School teacher can expect to commit about ten hours per month to this role: an hour each week to prepare, plus an hour each Sunday to teach, plus time in prayer, planning, and learning with other Sunday School teachers.

7. The teachers regularly participate in the monthly teachers meeting to increase their biblical knowledge and teaching skills.

Position Description

Teachers of the Faith are important members of the ministry team in our congregation because they have direct contact and influence with children, their parents, and other members of our congregation. These statements below will provide you with a sense of the task you are undertaking.

Teachers of the faith . . .

* serve for a period of one year, eligible for annual renewal.

* are to consider prayerfully every lesson as it is prepared to be taught.

* regard highly the spiritual needs of the children and their families entrusted to their care.

* strive to teach in ways that will promote the spiritual growth, health, and nurture of the children in the class.

* make the classroom space attractive and inviting for the learners.

* pray continually for their learners and for blessing upon the Sunday School programs.

* faithfully attend all training sessions and staff meetings offered for their benefit.

* arrive in their classrooms ten to fifteen minutes before the children arrive to be sure all is ready and to be able to focus on the individual children as they arrive.

* care for children and their families who are irregular in attendance, in cooperation with the pastor, elders, and Sunday School superintendent.

* supervise their students in any activities in which the students participate, such as singing in a worship service.

* become friends and counselors to their students. When possible, visit the homes of the students to use every means to establish rapport with the children and their families.

In recognition of the important role of Sunday School teachers in our congregation, we, the leaders of this congregation, pledge to . . .

* appoint teachers to their positions on the recommendation of the Sunday School superintendent or the Board of Christian Education with approval of our pastor and the elders.

* pray for the teachers in worship, staff meetings, and personal prayers.

* provide Christ-centered, Bible-based, and life-directed curriculum and related support materials in sufficient numbers for the students in the class.

* provide a budget line for teachers to secure additional teaching tools and related supplies for their classrooms.

* conduct regular teachers meetings that are timely, useful, and lead to a more effective Sunday School program.

* regularly feature information and articles about Sunday School in the church bulletin, newsletter, and Web site.

BASICS

Child Development

BY MARTHA STREUFERT JANDER

To be an effective Sunday School teacher, it helps to have a basic understanding of how young children develop. The four dimensions of learning include: physical, intellectual, social, and emotional development. Together, these dimensions fall under one overarching spiritual umbrella. Each dimension reflects and is grounded in the spiritual development of the individual child. Scripture tells us that Jesus grew as a "whole" child: "Jesus increased in wisdom and in stature and in favor with God and man" (Luke 2:52). Christ grew in wisdom (knowledge, insight, and judgment—gained through the fear of the Lord); in stature (physically); and in favor with God (spiritually) and man (socially and emotionally).

A child is born. The infant drinks milk. He or she cries and fusses to have needs met. The baby grows. The toddler begins to walk and talk and learn. The child learns to ask instead of crying for what they need. He learns to control his impulses. She learns to try again and again. The child grows taller and stronger. It knows to reach for what it wants. They learn that others have feelings and that to give and share is good and God-pleasing. Best of all, the child learns that he or she is a child of God, baptized into His family, forgiven and forgiving, growing to know God as Creator, Redeemer, and Sanctifier.

Each child grows and develops differently. They may learn one thing more quickly than another, or more adeptly than their peers. But all children must learn some things before the next step can be taken. They do not—indeed cannot—skip steps in their growing or their learning. Children must walk before they can run. They babble noises before their words are understood by others. They learn to say their names (at about age 2) before they can understand what separate letters mean (at ages 4–6). Before they can write words, children must have the small muscle control and eye-hand coordination to hold a crayon. Young children need to know that they can make marks on a paper before they can draw a circle (close to age 3). They must stack three blocks on top of each other before they can build a city of blocks.

Children must have their own needs met before they can recognize that others have needs as well. Before children can plan and form an object with clay or play dough, they need to play with and handle the clay. Children need to explore and discover what something is and what it does before they know what they can do with it. That's how God designed our human minds.

God fashions each child individually, in His own design. He loves each one, sent Jesus the Savior for each one, and by the power of the Holy Spirit in Holy Baptism creates faith in each one.

The reproducible charts found at the end of this chapter show the typical growth pattern for children spiritually, physically, intellectually, socially, emotionally, and in language development. Each chart describes the "typical" child between ages 2 and 8. Realize that some children at each age will fall well outside of the "norm."

Children of all ages need:

* Reassurance from adults when working or playing

* Unconditional love

* Unconditional acceptance

* Stability and sense of security

* Patience, assurance, and a listening ear from adults

* Models for initiating play and cooperative play

* To be given, or be reminded to use, words to express feelings

* Opportunities to play with other children

* Time to talk to, and with, others

Using Faith Words

Young children need to hear about God and how He acts in their lives, what He has done—and is doing—for them. In Deuteronomy 6:6–9, God tells His people through Moses to keep His Word always before them, to talk about Him along the way and when they sit down. God wanted them—as He wants us—to know Him through His Word, to trust Him, and to follow His plan for our life.

Intentional "faith talk" involves using the words of our faith tradition, found in the Bible, catechism, and hymnal as we speak about God. This involves planning in advance what you will tell children about God as they play with play dough, dress up at dramatic play, or work in groups at a project. Such intentional talk helps older children connect God's actions with their own lives as they hear about God when they talk and socialize.

The younger the children involved, the more they need to have hands-on experiences in order to understand the words you say. Research shows that children grow best when they are actively involved, when what they are doing is connected to what they hear. Learning centers help children grow physically, intellectually, socially, and emotionally, and will, with "faith talk," help them grow spiritually as well by the power of the Holy Spirit.

Self-Esteem

Much has been written about self-esteem in recent years. Studies have shown that children with "good" self-esteem have learned to do the right thing because it is the right thing to do, not because of any external reward they might get or even because of praise they might hear from others.

Children with positive self-esteem accept the gifts and talents God gives them as part of His design and plan for their lives. They begin to see and use these special abilities to the glory of God and for His Kingdom.

Christian children with high self-esteem have learned high "God-esteem." They know that they are children of God, made in His image, designed for His purpose, and that all they are and have is from God. Self-esteem grows as children learn that helping others is a good thing to do—not for any reward they might get—but because it pleases God and it is the right thing to do.

Each Child a Gift

As a Sunday School teacher or leader, you recognize that each child is a unique gift from God. He has gifted them with talents and abilities to be used in service to the Lord. As you work with these young gifted ones from God, help them grow in their understanding of God's Word and their role in the community of faith that we call the Church.

Comparing Child Development

The pages that follow contain a series of charts comparing children at various ages and stages of development. Realize that these are generalized statements and may not apply specifically to each individual child. The "real" children in your Sunday School may have abilities that fall well above or below the noted characteristics on these charts.

Two-year-olds

Spiritual

Transfer trust in people to trust in God.

Act out Bible stories with all children doing same action.

Listen to Bible stories.

Point to pictures of things God made as adult names them.

Fold hands during prayers.

Late: repeat simple prayers.

Respond with smiles, hugs when told "Jesus loves you."

Recognize pictures of Jesus.

Listen, clap, move during singing; may sing along.

Need assurance of adult's love and Jesus' love when left in strange place.

Physical

Early: draw lines on paper.

Late: draw circles.

Place stickers randomly.

Early: need help with 2/3 piece puzzles.

Late: do 4/5 piece puzzles alone.

Will stack 3 to 8 blocks.

Early: enjoy tearing paper.

Late: can cut with blunt scissors.

Move from using spoon to fork to other tools.

Late: string beads.

Go from stepping up one at a time to alternating feet.

Jump from low step to flat ground.

Turn pages of a book.

Intellectual

Learn through their senses.

Learn through exploring and experimenting.

Early: recognize some colors, shapes, and numbers.

Late: name some colors, shapes or numbers (may not until age 3 or 4).

Choose among activities set out for them.

Early: point to things in pictures.

Late: name things in pictures.

Recognize pictures with missing parts.

Enjoy big pictures in storytelling.

Match same-colored blocks.

Match shapes in objects and drawn on paper.

Late: sort completely different objects into groups.

Social/Emotional

Begin to think of themselves separate from important adults.

Want to "do it myself."

Know names of friends, other significant people.

Choose toys and entertain themselves.

Early: play next to other children.

Late: begin to play with others.

Pretend play with real-looking objects; pretend to do familiar activities.

Adapt well to class routines.

Easily comforted.

Late: begin to recognize feelings.

Tell adult of social needs.

Late: say if they are boy or girl.

Language

Early: use their first name.

Late: know first and last names.

Early: use two- to three-word sentences.

Late: ask questions with correct wording.

Early: answer yes/no questions.

Late: answer who, what, where questions.

Answer questions about body parts (What do you see with?).

Use simple pronouns (I, you, me), though not always correctly.

Do finger plays, action poems; act out Bible story.

Begin to count.

Repeat two unrelated words.

Early: may need demonstration of desired actions.

Late: follow two-step commands.

Late: use words like "mine," "under," "on."

Sunday School Basics © 2005 Concordia Publishing House. Reproduced by permission.

4

39

child development

BASICS

Three-year-olds

Spiritual

Say Jesus loves them, is their Friend.

Say God made them, takes care of them.

Express joy when hearing Jesus loves them.

Recognize others' sins against them but rarely see own sin.

Start to show a desire to love and obey God.

Say "I'm sorry" to God for bad things they do.

Worship enthusiastically, especially when singing (may use own words).

Know prayer is "talking to God;" can repeat or make up simple prayers.

Recognize Bible as God's Word; can repeat simple Bible verses.

Know they can tell about and show God's love to others.

Physical

Have more control of whole-body movement than at age 2.

Put on shoes but not tie; need little help to dress (buttons, zippers, ties).

Use toilet with some help; wash hands without help.

Run, jump, leap, march, climb, hop, balance, swing, throw balls overhand.

Scribble color; draw circles and squares.

Use glue sticks, place stickers with forethought.

Use blunt scissors to cut play dough, along lines, or long strips of paper.

Work puzzles (6-piece) by trial and error; string beads; build blocks to 10 in a tower.

Go upstairs alternating feet.

Enjoy working with play dough, but may not shape anything.

Intellectual

Know some colors, numbers, shapes; can tell/show differences in size, but cannot put in order.

In process of sorting out names and roles of people (may call all older men "Grandpa").

Solve immediate, interesting, concrete problems.

Draw pictures they can talk about and recognize; draw people with a few recognizable parts.

Cannot tell difference between fact and fantasy (magic/make-believe); believe everything is alive.

Enjoy listening to stories, rhymes.

Have short attention span; easily distracted.

Learn more through observing and doing than by adult teaching.

Begin to be aware of time concepts.

Think very literally/concretely (e.g., explain God in terms of own experience).

Social/Emotional

Seek attention and approval of adults.

Accept suggestions; follow simple directions.

Like to help with simple household tasks.

Make simple choices between two things.

Like to be silly and make others laugh.

Enjoy playing alone as well as with other children.

Unable to see things from another's viewpoint so have difficulty cooperating and sharing.

Watch and observe a good portion of time.

Like to pretend.

Interested in ethnic identities if exposed to other cultures.

Language

Say own name, age, street, and town.

Play with words: create rhyming words, say or make up words having similar sounds.

Enjoy repeating words and sounds.

May not have verbal skills to talk about what they know.

Talk in complete 3–5-word sentences; majority of speech can be understood.

Ask why and how questions.

May stumble over words at times.

May have trouble with verb tenses (bringed) and plurals (mouses).

Still learning many location words (under, through, over).

May experiment with unacceptable language.

Four-year-olds

Spiritual

Indicate feeling secure in God's love and care.

Express love for Jesus.

Express a desire to love and obey God.

Recognize others' sins against them, but do not always see own sin.

Ask God and those they've hurt for forgiveness.

Begin to repeat the Lord's Prayer, say own prayers, learn simple Bible verses.

Listen and participate in class worship, prayers, singing.

Show they feel part of God's family.

Begin to see that others need God's love.

Recognize that they can tell about and show God's love to others.

Physical

Have more whole-body movement and small muscle control than previously.

Gallop and slide; try to skip.

Enjoy movements that accompany songs.

Place stickers more accurately than previously.

Cut large shapes with blunt scissors.

Put 8–12-piece puzzle together; shapes figures with play dough.

May try to write name (with all capital letters).

Use toilet and washes hands without help.

Catch a bounced ball.

Go down steps by alternating feet.

Intellectual

Understand concepts like more, some, biggest, on, under, in.

May name 8–10 colors; 3 shapes; match them, tell them apart.

May count to 7 or more, not always in correct order.

Understand daily routines.

Beginning to understand time concepts (today, yesterday, tomorrow).

Confuse real and make-believe.

Use all senses in learning; like to explore and experiment with new materials.

Answer simple factual questions: what, who, when, how.

Follow picture directions set in sequence.

Place several story cards in correct sequence.

Social/Emotional

Plan things before carrying out: dramatic play, drawing pictures.

Complete tasks.

Relate stories to own life.

Listen quietly for up to five minutes in small/large group.

Get involved in acting out stories, dramatic play.

Often one child takes lead in play and others follow.

May be unsure in new situations, but more willing to have adventures on their own.

Loving, boastful, jealous, fearful, serious, or silly.

Beginning to get emotions under control; name basic emotions.

Still building a sense of self and need to "do it myself!"

Language

Use complex sentences.

Add "ed" to verbs: "I singed a song"; "He runned away."

Express needs and ideas in words.

Enjoy conversing about things that hold interest.

Question birth and death issues.

Ask/answer who, what, when, where, how, and why questions.

Enjoy nonsense words and silly rhymes.

Begin to recognize and name letters of the alphabet.

Recognize own name in print; may be able to print it.

May retell/narrate stories to go with their pictures.

Sunday School Basics © 2005 Concordia Publishing House. Reproduced by permission.

4

child development

Five-year-olds

Spiritual

Transfer trust in people to trust in God.

Will say Jesus loves them and others, that Jesus died for them.

View themselves as part of God's family.

Know sin needs to be punished; ask God to forgive them.

Can repeat the Ten Commandments, the Lord's Prayer; can learn simple Bible verses.

Know Jesus helps them.

Think of Jesus and God in physical terms.

Confuse terms God and Jesus.

Believe God loves people who do good and hates people who do wrong.

Say own (self-centered) prayers.

Physical

Run, hop, jump, gallop, begin to skip, throw and possibly catch a ball.

Prefer one hand over the other.

Have increased physical self-assurance and coordination.

May begin to lose, grow teeth.

Dress and undress with little help (can button and zip).

Tire easily.

Fall out of chairs easily—usually sideways.

Need to move and use large muscles.

Use fingers and hands for intricate skills.

Refining eye-hand coordination; finding right pencil grip.

Intellectual

Know name and address.

Predict what comes next using patterns.

Recognize and say letters of the alphabet without help.

May count to 100 and recognize numerals to 30.

Group up to four sets according to size, shape, color.

Retell stories and use pictures to tell a story.

Still separating real and pretend.

Plan and follow through with drawings, block building, dramatic play, and so forth.

Have a sense of order: what happened before/after.

Connect personal experiences with what goes on in world.

Social/Emotional

Feelings close to surface; express feelings physically.

More willing to take risks, but can be fearful about people, the dark, storms, and the like.

Want to be first; competitive; anxious to do well and win.

Need to know they are doing the right thing; failure is hard.

Critical of others; embarrassed by own mistakes.

Friends become important.

Enjoy dramatic play; able to negotiate roles, make up rules, and organize.

Identify people by their occupations.

Begin to realize that others have feelings, thoughts different from theirs.

Can be enthusiastic, bossy, teasing, sometimes dishonest.

Language

Very literal in thinking (everything is as you say).

Enjoy talking to others about things in which they are interested.

Think aloud.

Give verbal instructions to themselves as they perform tasks.

Will answer last question first.

Explain and describe what they know using informal language.

Enjoy jokes and riddles.

Learning to listen and respond to others.

May know or learn that letters have sounds and associate sounds with written symbols.

May use unacceptable language for attention.

Six-year-olds

Spiritual

Believe God made them and cares for them; know Jesus is their Friend and Savior.

Recognize right from wrong but not always in themselves.

Begin to see sin in themselves and know they need a Savior.

Ask for forgiveness from Jesus and from friends they've hurt.

Want to love and obey God.

Know difference between God the Father and Jesus; begin to know the Holy Spirit and what He does.

Say the Lord's Prayer; learn the Ten Commandments; make up their own prayers.

Like to act out Bible stories or have them presented in different ways.

Know the Bible as God's Word and that it is true because God says so.

Express a desire to tell others about Jesus and His love for all people.

Physical

Polishing skills learned in kindergarten: cutting, gluing, drawing, and so forth.

Lose, grow teeth.

More small muscle control/coordination evident, but not all can tie shoes.

Print name/alphabet.

Run, hop, skip, jump, slide, balance.

Become adept at throwing, catching, kicking balls—small and large.

Chew on things: pencils, erasers, hair; fall out of chairs easily.

Increased visual discrimination.

Lots of energy and drive—more work, but sloppier—speed is essential.

Can be ill frequently.

Intellectual

Learn how to learn: to read, write, spell, take tests, and the like.

Get reality and fiction confused; may believe because they think it, it's true.

Tell difference between "real" and "fantasy"; interested in magic.

Begin to recognize sequence of (Bible) stories; understand more about past, present, future.

Able to hold images in their minds for longer time periods; ready for "sit-down" learning.

Longer attention spans—can work until project is finished.

Become so absorbed in project it's difficult to move on; or be in a hurry to get done.

Enjoy reading, being read to, retelling stories or predicting.

Learn best by doing and being involved.

Express themselves in artistic ways; new ways always intriguing.

Social

Friends important, but best friends may change often; may also have "worst enemy."

Enjoy working with friends on projects, in dramatic play, and so forth.

Want to do all things right and excel at everything.

Enjoy board and outdoor games; concerned about fair play and following rules.

Enjoy jokes and riddles.

Still want to do "show and tell."

Can be bossy, teasing, complaining, stubborn.

Cooperative play at its best; love dramatic play.

Begin to know other people may think differently from themselves.

Classrooms can be noisy.

Emotional

Emotions lie close to surface; get feelings hurt easily; moods can change often and quickly.

May have imaginary or real fears.

Take criticism and failure hard: how adults use words extremely important.

Excitable and excited, compulsive, dawdlers but want to be first.

Tattle as a form of keeping things in balance.

Struggle with control: want to do it but look for affirmation and assurance and help.

Need swift appropriate consequences when rules are not followed.

Become easily worried about easily explained things.

View everything in extremes; very little middle ground.

Lie at times to stay out of trouble: want to be seen only as good; may say "I was only teasing."

Ready for responsibility in cleaning, getting work done.

Language

Like to explain things and want someone to listen as they do.

Can carry on discussions and conversations.

Use inventive spelling, write about things they know.

Reversal of letters common.

Use words they know to replace words they don't know.

May find it difficult to follow more than one or two directions at a time.

Know to read from top to bottom, from left to right.

Tell a story from a picture, but can't always write it down.

Connect and compare what they hear and read with their own and with experiences of others.

Predict and draw conclusions from what they hear, read.

Sunday School Basics © 2005 Concordia Publishing House. Reproduced by permission.

Seven-year-olds

Spiritual

Know God the Father as Creator, Jesus as Savior, the Spirit as Giver of faith and gifts.

Know God loves and cares for them, forgives them.

Express love for God/Jesus.

Know when they do wrong; can ask for forgiveness from God and from friends.

Believe sin needs to be punished.

Know the Ten Commandments, the Lord's Prayer, the Apostles' Creed.

Know Satan is evil and wants to keep us from knowing God's love.

Ask God to help them and to change their hearts.

Begin to understand that through Baptism, God makes them His children.

Pray for others and want to tell others about Jesus.

Physical

Active and full of energy.

Can be physically active for long periods.

Jump rope, hold balance, clap accurately in rhythm.

Catch, throw, kick, bounce, dribble balls with accuracy.

Participate in team sports.

More ability to do detailed tasks using small muscles.

Know about their body and how it works.

Vision more nearsighted, so works closely to paper; copying from board often difficult.

Know how to use equipment and space safely.

More aware of health issues for self and family members.

Intellectual

Have high expectations of themselves.

Strive for perfection; erase a lot to achieve that.

May quit if they see perfection is not doable; need to experience success.

Evaluate themselves by what others are doing.

May be in such deep thought they truly don't hear.

Enjoy reading.

Want to see how things work.

Need closure on tasks, to complete assignments.

Enjoy board games, manipulatives.

Want to work alone in small spaces and to repeat tasks.

Social

Increased sense of themselves and their role in the world; can be critical of themselves.

Increased sensitivity to others.

May withdraw as they sort and think about things in their own minds.

Can be seen as moody, shy, or withdrawn.

Want to make friends, but friendships change often.

Seek acceptance of peers.

Talk to impress adults, want their approval.

May feel everyone is against them.

Can exaggerate.

Enjoy being helpers.

Emotional

Live close to tears, but enjoy humor.

Feelings often changeable.

Worry about things happening in the world.

Can be anxious about friendships, schoolwork, new situations.

Have strong likes, dislikes.

Need constant encouragement.

May pull back when overwhelmed with things they think they can't handle.

Don't like when things change; need to know when routines change.

Need security and structure in routines.

Want things to be perfect; discouraged when it doesn't happen.

Language

Read and write independently.

Read more fluently with expression.

Are good listeners; can evaluate and ask good questions.

Like to talk on one-to-one basis.

Vocabulary development expanding quickly.

Interested in the meaning of words.

Learn to use dictionaries and other reference materials.

Like to write and send notes.

Writing becomes more legible.

Like codes and puzzles involving words.

Eight-year-olds

Spiritual

Praise God for who He is: all-knowing, present everywhere, forgiving, loving.

Tell of God's plan to send Jesus as the Savior.

Confess their sins, knowing God forgives them for Jesus' sake.

Know Jesus is God and yet is human.

Know and say the Ten Commandments, the Lord's Prayer, the Apostles' Creed.

Describe the work of the Holy Spirit.

Express trust in God to take care of their physical and spiritual needs.

Thank God for His love and care.

Ask for forgiveness from God and from those they hurt; forgive those who have hurt them.

Want to tell others about Jesus, their Savior.

Intellectual

May have difficulty organizing work.

Work hard and quickly.

Work well in a group.

Still need hands-on, explorative learning.

Feel competent at skills.

May take on more than they are capable of doing.

Improving in all areas of reading, writing, spelling.

Developing an interest in logic and the "why" of rules.

Interested in nature, in how things work and are put together.

Increased reading of chapter books; enjoy mythology, fantasy.

Physical

Tire easily but come back with a bounce.

Vision strong enough to see near and far; can now copy from chalkboard easily.

Lots of energy; need outside time.

Can be awkward as they go through growth spurts.

Physically able to master cursive writing.

Frequent exercise or breaks needed to help them concentrate.

Can jump and land, jump rope, jog, do other physical activities with good control.

Can mirror a partner's actions.

Can identify foods, health habits that advance/deter a healthy body.

Learn to accept physical limitations in self and others.

Social

Social and friendly.

Prefer own gender groups; sometimes very large groups.

May exclude others in forming "clubs."

Have strong sense of fairness in play, sports, games.

Recognize responsibility in helping others.

Have strong interest in other cultures and people.

Enjoy dramatic play, where they can be a character they know.

Make up rules for old games or invent new games.

Will challenge limitations and boundaries.

Feel competent at basic skills, but inferior when looking at what all they don't know.

Emotional

Need opportunity to practice new social skills.

Become critical of others, especially their mother.

Can be rude and argumentative.

Exaggerate their own abilities.

Have hard time dealing with criticism and failure.

Losing in games not as traumatic as it once was.

Less sensitive and withdrawn than at 7; recover quickly from mistakes.

Begin to have overall sense of knowing worth as God's children.

Concerned with fairness and justice.

Have learned to wait for most things, but can be impatient waiting for special days or events.

Language

Enjoy riddles, knock-knock jokes, humor, word puzzles; enjoy talk, gossip.

Can converse easily with peers and adults.

Bursting with great ideas; eager to tell them.

Reading, writing, and spelling skills always improving.

Use descriptive words in writing; writing longer pieces in different genres.

May be writing or learning to write in cursive.

Speaking skills improve; grammar improves.

Tell the difference between fact and fiction.

Summarize, interpret, evaluate what they hear/read.

Know that language can reflect family and culture.

Sunday School Basics © 2005 Concordia Publishing House. Reproduced by permission.

Reviewing Curriculum

BY JOHN PLESS

Introduction

Curriculum serves as a key ingredient in the recipe for good Sunday School. Features of a curriculum are multifaceted. Attractiveness and adaptability rank high on the list of characteristics that Sunday School staff members often consider in reviewing proposed material. As important as these characteristics sound, there remains yet a more essential issue—the truthfulness and clarity in the presentation of God's Word. This chapter seeks to offer some theological guidelines that pastors and other congregational leaders should use in discerning whether or not to utilize a particular curriculum in the Lutheran Sunday School. Diagnostic questions are included after each section to help you analyze a given curriculum. (If you or a team wish to review a curriculum, copy the questions on p. 55.)

A Primary Distinction

The Bible cannot be rightly understood without a proper distinction between God's Law and His Gospel. Material that blurs this distinction will confuse learners leading them either into despair over their inability to keep God's commandments or into an attitude of spiritual smugness and self-righteousness. Holy Scripture teaches us that God speaks two messages to human beings, His Law and His Gospel (Romans

3:19–31). This twofold speaking of God is reflected in the Lutheran Confessions: "All Scripture should be divided into these two chief doctrines, the law and the promises. In some places it presents the law. In others it presents the promise of Christ; this it does either when it promises that the Messiah will come and promises forgiveness of sins, justification, and eternal life for His sake, or when, in the New Testament, the Christ who came promises forgiveness of sins, justification, and eternal life" (*Book of Concord,* p. 108). The Law includes all the demands that God makes on human beings and the threat of punishment that falls on those who fail to fear, love and trust in Him above all things. The Law is summarized in the Ten Commandments but is not limited to them. By contrast, the Gospel is that Word of God in which He promises to forgive sins, bless with new life, and bestow eternal life for the sake of Christ Jesus. We receive the Gospel by faith alone, apart from any human work (Ephesians 2:8–9).

In evaluating Sunday School materials, the crucial element we look for is the Gospel quotient of the lessons. Both Law and Gospel are necessary. Without the Law, the Gospel will collapse into a generic philosophy of tolerance and acceptance; it becomes confused with a generic declaration of God's love. Without the Gospel, the Law will crush with its unrelenting demands. The Gospel can never be assumed. It must be carefully articulated as it declares that God in Christ reconciled the world to Himself through the blood of Jesus Christ shed on the cross (2 Corinthians 5:16–21; Colossians 1:15–23; 1 Timothy 1:12–17). The Gospel—not the Law—contains the power of God for salvation and the life of faith (Romans 1:16–17).

A clear sign of the muddling of the Law and the Gospel is seen in statements that suggest salvation to be a matter of human choice or decision. The curriculum coming from many American evangelical publishers state that the goal of the lesson involves evoking in the student a decision to accept Jesus as his or her Lord and Savior. This approach ignores the biblical truth that sinners are spiritually dead and therefore incapable of doing anything including "inviting Jesus into my life" to bring about their salvation. When it comes to salvation, God does it all (Ephesians 2:1–7).

Diagnostic Questions:

* *Does the material clearly distinguish between what God demands (Law) and what He gives (Gospel)?*

* *Does the material clearly distinguish between justification (God's work of declaring sinners righteous for the sake of Christ's atoning work) and sanctification (the ongoing struggle to put the old Adam to death)?*

* *Does the material attempt to coerce, cajole, or challenge believers to a life of obedience or does it set forth Christ Jesus, crucified and risen from the dead, as the center and foundation for the Christian life (Galatians 2:20; Colossians 2:7)?*

* Is Jesus Christ portrayed as an example or coach or as our Savior? Christ as example, coach, or enabler still leaves students in the realm of the Law. Sinners do not need a moral teacher, guide, or example, but a Savior. A faithful Sunday School curriculum will anchor students' confidence not in themselves and their efforts but in the free gift of salvation won for us by Christ alone.

* Does the material contain the language of "decision theology"?

How Does the Curriculum Use the Bible?

In evaluating Sunday School curriculum we should pay close attention to how the material treats the Holy Scriptures. The prophetic and apostolic Scriptures alone contain *the* source for all that we say of God and His will. The Bible alone serves as the norm or yardstick used to measure all teachings in the Church (2 Peter 1:16–21; 2 Timothy 3:14–17). The Bible is not set alongside of tradition, reason, or experience as a source of authority for Christian believing and living. We rightly attend to the Word of God only when we put ourselves under His Word and receive from God what He gives us in the words that His Spirit caused to be written for our learning. The Bible does not exist as an artifact of human religious thinking to be interpreted or used according to perceived cultural or individual needs. Any material that questions the reliability of the Holy Scriptures undermines the goal of all genuine Christian education—saving faith in the Lord Jesus Christ.

It is not enough that a curriculum asserts the inerrancy of Scripture. Many religious groups make the claim that the Bible is true. They even agree that the Bible contains the only source of Christian teaching. Yet many misinterpret or fail to understand the Scriptures and so miss what Scripture actually teaches about Christ and His gifts. Solid Sunday School materials not only confess that the Bible is God's infallible Word, but they also demonstrate how the Scriptures must be rightly interpreted according to the mind of the Spirit who inspired them. This means that the curriculum should be guided by sound principles of biblical interpretation. Questions like "What do you think this passage means?" or "What does this story mean to you?" become subjective and divert learners from what God actually says in the text. The material should contain questions and exercises that engage the student with the biblical text, providing him or her with the opportunity to grow in their knowledge of the Bible and in the skill of properly interpreting the Scriptures.

Diagnostic Questions:

* Is the Bible understood to be the inerrant Word of God or is it seen simply as an elevated form of religious literature that perhaps contains or bears witness to God's Word?

* How does the material understand the clarity of the Scriptures? Does the material show that Jesus Christ is the light of the world and it is only in

and through Him that the Scriptures are clear (John 8:12; Luke 24:25–27)?

* Does the material allow "Scripture to interpret Scripture"?

* Is the efficacy of the Scripture—the ability of the Scripture to do what it promises—clearly taught (Isaiah 55:11; John 6:63; John 20:30–31) or is the Bible seen as a collection of spiritual principles that Christians must now implement?

* Is a reliable and accurate translation of the Bible consistently employed throughout the curriculum?

Where Do Baptism and the Lord's Supper Fit in the Curriculum?

The Lord Jesus Christ instituted Baptism (Matthew 28:19–20) as the means for granting us the forgiveness of sins (Acts 2:38–39), the new birth of the Spirit (John 3:5–6; Titus 3:5–7), and deliverance from death and the devil (Romans 6:3–5; Galatians 3:27; 1 Peter 3:21). Baptism is not a human act of commitment like the Pledge of Allegiance. Rather Baptism involves solely the work of God. In Baptism, He claims sinners as His own with His name and clothes them with His blood-bought righteousness. God intends Baptism for all people without regard to age.

On the night of His betrayal, the Lord Jesus established the Holy Supper of His body and blood (Matthew 26:26–28; 1 Corinthians 11:23–26). In this Sacrament Christ gives us His body to eat and His blood to drink under the bread and wine. The Lord's Supper serves not as a sacrifice that the Church offers to God, nor as a dramatic reenactment used to memorialize a past event. The Lord's Supper belongs not to the Christian but to Christ. It exists not as a party that the Church puts on for Jesus. It is the meal of the New Testament, the gift of Jesus' body and blood given us to eat and to drink as the pledge that the forgiveness won at Calvary is for us. The Supper delivers Christ's own gifts of forgiveness of sins, life, and salvation to those who repent and trust in His gracious promises.

Departing from the teaching of God's Word, some make Baptism a human rite of initiation into a church or identification with Christ. Such teaching robs Baptism of all that the Scripture teaches us concerning the power God places in this Sacrament. Likewise, some push the Lord's Supper to the edge of the church's life, reducing it to a meal that Christians partake of in the memory of Christ. Some Christian publishers elect not to treat the sacraments at all, or in a marginal way, in order to appeal to the widest possible audience. Lutherans find these approaches to the sacraments in Sunday School curriculum to be completely unacceptable. Our Lord commands His Church to teach all things (Matthew 28:20) He gave us. The sacraments are not an optional element in Sunday School curriculum.

Diagnostic Questions:

* *What does the curriculum teach about the institution and benefit of Baptism and the Lord's Supper?*

* *Are the sacraments omitted or minimized in the curriculum?*

* *Are the sacraments understood as the work and gift of Christ or are they seen as rituals performed by Christians?*

* *What is taught about the Baptism of infants?*

* *Is the Lord's Supper understood in a symbolic fashion?*

How Does the Curriculum Connect to the Catechism?

Paul exhorted Timothy to "follow the pattern of sound words that you have heard from me, in the faith and love that are in Christ Jesus" (2 Timothy 1:13). The Small Catechism was prepared by Martin Luther to be just such a pattern of sound words. Early Lutherans even called the catechism " 'The layman's Bible' [containing] everything which Holy Scripture discusses at greater length and which a Christian must know for his salvation" (*Book of Concord*, p. 465). The Ten Commandments, the Apostles' Creed, and the Lord's Prayer, all drawn from the Scriptures, form the core of the catechism. Luther adds Baptism and the Lord's Supper, anchoring both in the words of Jesus (who instituted them), while unpacking their benefits and tutoring us in how faith receives these gifts. In time, Luther would also insert a short form of Confession between Baptism and the Sacrament of the Altar. Our duty "to thank and praise, serve and obey" (Small Catechism, p. 14) gains concrete form in the daily prayers and the table of duties appended to the catechism. God's Law (Ten Commandments) shows us our sin. The Apostles' Creed embodies the Gospel of the triune God. Faith calls on the Father in the words His Son gave us to pray (Lord's Prayer). Faith receives the gifts Jesus designates in Baptism, in the words of the Absolution, and with His body and blood in the Lord's Supper. Lives made holy by the Spirit are lived in the "holy orders" of congregation, community, and home. The catechism shows us repentance, faith, and holy living.

A Lutheran Sunday School will benefit by using a curriculum that incorporates the catechism into the lessons at a level appropriate to each age group. In this way, the catechism will be seen as a book to be utilized throughout the life of the Christian and not simply as a textbook for confirmation instruction. Using the catechism in the Sunday School assists in laying the foundation for more substantial catechesis both in confirmation class and throughout your students' lives. A good curriculum draws out connections between the biblical narrative and chief parts of Christian doctrine embodied in the catechism.

In the Preface to the Small Catechism, Luther laid out a threefold plan for teaching the faith. Luther urged pastors and parents to (1) avoid variations in the basic texts, (2) teach the text itself, (3) and then teach what the text means. Then once people have mastered the Small Catechism they may take up the Large Catechism. Luther's principles remain sturdy, didactic guides. A good curriculum assists students in learning key texts by heart and growing in their understanding and application of these texts.

Diagnostic Questions:

* Are portions of the catechism related to individual lessons? For example, does a unit on prayer incorporate the explanations of the Lord's Prayer from the catechism?

* Does the curriculum make provision for learning parts of the catechism by heart in a way that is appropriate to the age level of the student?

How Are Liturgy and Hymnody Incorporated into the Curriculum?

Our teaching is drawn from the Scripture, confessed in the catechism, and expressed in the hymnal. A good Sunday School curriculum facilitates the use of all three books. The curriculum should assist teachers in drawing connections with the liturgy and hymnody of the Church. In this way, the Sunday School both presupposes the divine service and leads children back into the liturgical life of the Church with a greater awareness of what our Lord Jesus Christ does through His Word and Sacrament.

The curriculum should bring elements of the liturgy into the classroom. Material should incorporate liturgical responses, hymns, and collects for actual worship within the classroom. In this way, the Sunday School prepares and deepens each student's ability to participate in the church service. Lectionary-based lessons coordinated with the Church Year work well as the Sunday School reinforces themes that the student hears in worship.

Repetition and predictability help link Sunday School with the liturgy. A curriculum that employs solid hymns blesses children with an ever-increasing treasury of songs that accompanies them throughout their lives.

Hymns not only express the faith; they teach it. A good curriculum avoids trendy songs without Christ-centered substance. A good rule of thumb states that we ought never teach children something that they must later unlearn. The best approach is found in a curriculum that provides opportunities for the student to grow into the hymnody of the Church at an age-appropriate level.

Diagnostic Questions:

* Does the material utilize Lutheran liturgy and hymnody?

* What provisions are made for worship within the classroom?

* To what extent are the lessons coordinated with the Church Year?

How Does the Curriculum Teach Christian Vocation?

The Christian life has a dual focus. To borrow the language of Luther, Christians live outside of themselves in Christ by faith and in the neighbor by love. Being comes before doing. We are not saved by our love but through faith in Jesus Christ. Our good works do not make us Christian, but the Christian is busy and active in a life of good works. God does not need our good works, but the world does. The life of good works is lived out in the place of our calling—in the family, congregation, community, and workplace. Freed by the Gospel, the Christian now lives a life of service not in order to gain salvation, but to serve the well-being of the neighbor. The Christian life is not one of achievement and self-fulfillment but of servanthood.

Called into Christ's royal priesthood by Baptism (1 Peter 2:9–10), the Christian lives to offer spiritual sacrifices (1 Peter 2:4–5; Romans 12:1–2) in the world. These sacrifices do not merit God's favor but are sacrifices of thanksgiving expressed by the lip and the life of the Christian.

For all of God's unmerited goodness to us, we "thank, praise, serve and obey" Him to use the language of the catechism. Or to use the words of Paul:

> And let the peace of Christ rule in your hearts, to which indeed you were called in one body. And be thankful. Let the word of Christ dwell in you richly, teaching and admonishing one another in all wisdom, singing psalms and hymns and spiritual songs, with thankfulness in your hearts to God. And whatever you do, in word or deed, do everything in the name of the Lord Jesus, giving thanks to God the Father through Him. Colossians 3:15–17

It is essential that the distinction between being and doing, grace and works, faith and love be clearly articulated in the curriculum. Only then can we avoid moralism with students firmly anchored in the saving Gospel of Jesus Christ. The curriculum should give evidence of applications not only in Church life but also in the realms of family, citizenship, and the workplace.

Diagnostic Questions:

* How does the curriculum express the doctrine of vocation?

* Are good works seen as a fruit of faith directed toward the neighbor or is the Christian life portrayed in a moralistic fashion?

* Are the applications chiefly in the area of "church work"?

* Does the material distinguish between the royal priesthood and the office of the holy ministry? Does the material contain references to women serving as pastors (1 Corinthians 14:33–35; 1 Timothy 2:11–14)?

Adapting Curriculum

Even the most well-written, biblically accurate curriculum may still need adaptation to fit your congregation's specific situation. The reality of the number of students in your Sunday School could require combining two or even more grades. Some Sunday Schools are so small that they require only one teacher. By contrast some Sunday Schools are so large that they may have multiple classrooms of the same-age students. In each of these cases it is helpful to choose a curriculum that offers flexibility. Look for curriculums that offer levels that allow flexibility concerning grade levels. The best materials are divided more by students' reading abilities rather than specific grade levels. Don't be afraid to use the materials for a lower or higher level if they are a better fit for your specific group of students.

A unified curriculum, where all levels of students are studying the same Bible text or story, allows for greater adaptation, especially by the small Sunday School. The teacher needs only to prepare to teach one story, while adapting materials for two or three levels of students.

For the larger Sunday School, consider materials that offer the flexibility of use in a Large Group/Small Group format. In this case, you need materials that follow the same Bible story or text as well as the same sequence of steps across a number of grade levels. This allows one or more "master teachers" to tell the Bible story with the large group, while small-group leaders do the follow-up questions and activities with their small groups.

Don't be afraid to enlist the assistance of a professional educator or your director of Christian education when making curriculum choices or adapting a curriculum. Their training and background could prove particularly helpful in adapting a curriculum for your church's Sunday School.

Conclusion

The goal of careful evaluation of proposed Sunday School curriculum is to let the Word of God have free course so that Christ's lambs are fed with His precious Gospel, built up in the true faith, guarded from destructive teaching, and equipped for their vocation in the world as baptized children of the heavenly Father.

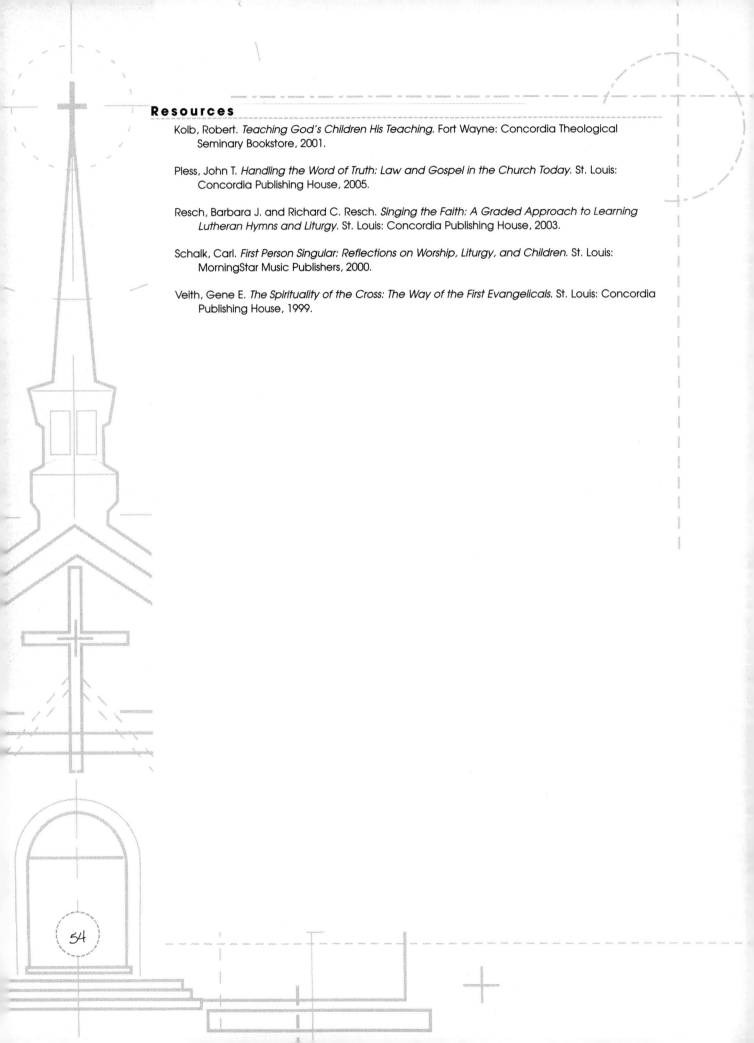

Resources

Kolb, Robert. *Teaching God's Children His Teaching*. Fort Wayne: Concordia Theological Seminary Bookstore, 2001.

Pless, John T. *Handling the Word of Truth: Law and Gospel in the Church Today*. St. Louis: Concordia Publishing House, 2005.

Resch, Barbara J. and Richard C. Resch. *Singing the Faith: A Graded Approach to Learning Lutheran Hymns and Liturgy*. St. Louis: Concordia Publishing House, 2003.

Schalk, Carl. *First Person Singular: Reflections on Worship, Liturgy, and Children*. St. Louis: MorningStar Music Publishers, 2000.

Veith, Gene E. *The Spirituality of the Cross: The Way of the First Evangelicals*. St. Louis: Concordia Publishing House, 1999.

* Does the material clearly distinguish between what God demands (Law) and what He gives (Gospel)?

* Does the material clearly distinguish between justification (God's work of declaring sinners righteous for the sake of Christ's atoning work) and sanctification (the ongoing struggle to put the old Adam to death)?

* Does the material attempt to coerce, cajole, or challenge believers to a life of obedience or does it set forth Christ Jesus, crucified and risen from the dead, as the center and foundation for the Christian life?

* Is Jesus Christ portrayed as an example or coach or as our Savior?

* Does the material contain the language of "decision theology"?

* Is the Bible understood to be the inerrant Word of God or is it seen simply as an elevated form of religious literature that perhaps contains or bears witness to God's Word?

* How does the material understand the clarity of the Scriptures? Does the material show that Jesus Christ is the light of the world and it is only in and through Him that the Scriptures are clear?

* Does the material allow "Scripture to interpret Scripture"?

* Is the efficacy of the Scripture—the ability of the Scripture to do what it promises—clearly taught or is the Bible seen as a collection of spiritual principles that Christians must now implement?

* Is a reliable and accurate translation of the Bible consistently employed throughout the curriculum?

* What does the curriculum teach about the institution and benefit of Baptism and the Lord's Supper?

* Are the sacraments omitted or minimized in the curriculum?

* Are the sacraments understood as the work and gift of Christ or are they seen as rituals performed by Christians?

* What is taught about the Baptism of infants?

* Is the Lord's Supper understood in a symbolic fashion?

* Are portions of the catechism related to individual lessons? For example, does a unit on prayer incorporate the explanations of the Lord's Prayer from the catechism?

* Does the curriculum make provision for learning parts of the catechism by heart in a way that is appropriate to the age level of the student?

* Does the material utilize Lutheran liturgy and hymnody?

* What provisions are made for worship within the classroom?

* To what extent are the lessons coordinated with the Church Year?

* How does the curriculum express the doctrine of vocation?

* Are good works seen as a fruit of faith directed toward the neighbor or is the Christian life portrayed in a moralistic fashion?

* Are the applications chiefly in the area of "church work"?

* Does the material distinguish between the royal priesthood and the office of the holy ministry? Does the material contain references to women serving as pastors (1 Corinthians 14:33–35; 1 Timothy 2:11–14)?

Sunday School Basics © 2005 Concordia Publishing House. Reprinted by permission.

Structuring Your Sunday School

BY WILLIAM G. MOORHEAD

What's Structure?

To structure something gives it form or arrangement. In psychology, structure refers to the organization of both one's external and internal environment. Architecturally, structure refers to a building or a national monument, such as the Gateway Arch on the riverfront in St. Louis or the Statue of Liberty in New York Harbor, or the landscaping around a private residence or business. Structure can even refer to the rules for personal and behavioral boundaries which are established, known, and honored, whether at home, work, or school. The Tower of Babel (Genesis 11:1–9) was a structure ancient people built to attempt to reach heaven and control God. In Matthew 7:24–27, Jesus teaches a parable warning His followers not to build a structure (faith) on sand. In Luke 14:25–33, Jesus, in teaching the meaning of discipleship, warns His followers to count the cost before building something in order to avoid the humiliation of not being able to finish it (and having the unfinished structure be a constant sign of failure). Jesus even references an event of His day—the collapse of the Tower in Siloam, which killed eighteen people (Luke 13:4)—to impress upon His disciples the need to repent. The evangelist Mark tells us that the disciples, just like tourists today, were in awe of the impressive structures in Jerusalem (see

Mark 13:1). Jesus' response indicates that He was less impressed with the structures and more impressed with what God was up to (Mark 13:2–37).

Sunday School Structure

If, as is generally and often asserted, the decline of the Sunday School is one of the worst kept secrets in the Church, could it be that structure, or more importantly, failure to implement a proper structure is partly to blame? A structure like the Washington Monument has changed little if at all since it was built. But then, tourists don't care that such a monument doesn't change. Monuments are not supposed to change—most tourists would be greatly disappointed if they did.

Sunday School, too, has changed little down through the years. Yet your Sunday School might benefit from a structural analysis, maybe even a change of structure. To structure a Sunday School, one decides what elements, or parts, would create a functioning, cohesive whole, and arranges them accordingly in light of the overall purpose or goal. Just as the builder of a house needs blueprints or at least knowledge of what the owner wants in the house, so the structure of a Sunday School needs a plan that is carefully thought out and prayed over regarding how best to achieve the congregation's educational ministry goals.

Just as some people don't want multilevel homes with lots of steps because they would not suit their current circumstances, so a congregation and those responsible for the congregation's educational ministry must know where they are headed, or want to head, in order to structure something that will help get them there. Ministry goals define direction and help leaders make decisions regarding what to include in or exclude from the structure or model. As someone I know once said, "If you don't know where you're going, you'll end up somewhere else!" That happens in a lot of Sunday Schools, maybe even in yours. But it doesn't have to!

Four Models

There are essentially four basic models for structuring the Sunday School. Each is briefly described and "visited" here. Elements of these four models can be blended to suit your congregation's circumstances.

Traditional Model

The traditional model is—well—traditional. In many ways it is not entirely different from the structure used for most elementary schools. While some people have been critical of the traditional model in recent years, it is by far the most widely used model for Sunday School. Visit this Sunday School and here is what you will most likely find:

1. *Students generally stay in separate, structured, grade-level classrooms for the entire period.*

2. *One teacher (or possibly a team of two) is responsible for preparing and teaching all the material, including the Bible story, art, music, and other suggested activities.*

3. *Student interaction with other teachers or other classes is limited.*

4. *Students usually interact only with their teacher and the students in their classroom.*

5. *Curriculum material supplied to each student.*

6. *Teaching depends heavily on the presentation style of the teacher.*

7. *A different Bible story or concept each week (often called the lectionary method), usually, but not always, correlated with the Scripture readings in worship that Sunday.*

Site Rotation Model

This model does what its name implies: students, either the same age or in mixed-age groups, visit a number of different locations within the building or on the premises (possibly even off premises) in order to learn the Bible story, do crafts, sing music, play games, make snacks, or participate in other creative, hands-on learning experiences. A visit to this Sunday School will show:

1. *Students of various ages interacting with one another throughout the lesson.*

2. *Teachers preparing and teaching activities they are most comfortable with or skilled at.*

3. *Classroom space dedicated to the type of activity that happens there (music, drama, art, story, video, crafts).*

4. *A different Bible story or concept every week or almost every week.*

5. *A more relaxed atmosphere.*

Rotation Model

According to this model, students in mixed-age groups experience the same Bible story, perhaps as often as four or five times in a four- or five-week rotation cycle. Each week the perspective or medium is different: art, drama, audiovisual, computers, games, music, puppets, and life skills, for example (in a five-week rotation not all perspectives will be used). If you visit this Sunday School you will see and experience:

1. *Bible stories and concepts taught in the same workshops over the course of four or five weeks, rotating the students to a different workshop each week.*

2. *A teacher, or team of teachers, lead the same workshop each week.*

3. *A more relaxed and interactive atmosphere.*

4. *A "rotation" period where only one Bible story is taught throughout the cycle—as opposed to the lectionary system where a different story is taught each week.*

5. *Classrooms designed according to the media and activities being employed in them.*

Note: in this model you will likely need teams writing lesson plans for each workshop, a volunteer coordinator, a supplies coordinator, and a worship leader. A team or teams will also choose the ten Bible stories to be studied each year. In choosing the biblical material you will want to rely heavily on your pastor and other education professionals in your congregation.

Large Group/Small Group Model

With this model, the Sunday School convenes as one large group, or possibly several larger groups, depending on the overall size of the Sunday School, for the opening and teaching of the Bible story. Crafts, discussion, music, drama, prayer, and other activities are done in smaller groups. Sometimes students break into age-level groups for further learning. The session may or may not conclude in one large group. Group size is driven by the activity planned. Some activities are done in larger groups, some in smaller. In some respects this model is a variant of both the site rotation and rotation models. However, the dynamic of this model is that throughout the session students may find themselves in different groups of varying sizes. A visitor to a Sunday School using this model will likely notice:

1. *Educational groupings of mixed ages and varying sizes.*

2. *A teacher or teaching team working more in areas of expertise and comfort level.*

3. *Configuring and reconfiguring groups throughout the period according to the type of activity.*

4. *Again, a more relaxed and interactive atmosphere.*

5. *More interaction among all participants.*

6. *A mixture of teaching styles.*

Pros and Cons

Every model has advantages and disadvantages. As you consider the structure of each of these four models, answer these questions for yourself:

* *Which model best lends itself to teaching God's plan of salvation as revealed in the Bible?*

Which model, if any, lends itself to teaching solid Lutheran doctrine and theology?

Can you list pros and cons for each of the four models we have just discussed?

In which model would your students likely learn better?

Do certain age groups do better with certain models?

For which model would it be easiest to recruit volunteers?

For which model are our present facilities most suited?

What changes in facilities can we make to accommodate the model we desire?

How will the educationally challenged be accommodated in the chosen model?

How will we measure success? By increased attendance? By the addition of new families?

What kind of volunteer staff will be required?

Which model requires more budget dollars?

Are any of the models used in congregations nearby so that we can talk to someone about their experiences?

Who Will Make the Structure Decision?

The most basic decision-making team usually consists of the pastor and Sunday School superintendent. Beyond that it will depend on who else is involved in the congregation's educational enterprises. A director of Christian education? A Board of Education? Lay volunteer teachers? Other called education professionals? The more people you can involve in the process, the better.

Sometimes all Sunday School leaders want and need is supportive families and excited and attending students. Just evaluate your structure with that in mind. Draw families who are active as well as those who are inactive into the evaluation process.

Okay, Now What?

Now you get to ask challenging questions.

1. *What is the overall purpose of your Sunday School?*

2. *Which of the four models will best serve your purpose?*

3. *What must we change or eliminate?*

4. *What must you keep?*

5. *What must we begin to do or do differently?*

6. *How will these decisions impact budget, space needs, recruitment of volunteers, material needs, and so forth?*

7. *Who can help us?*

As you ponder these questions take a look at the following factors as you get started.

Physical Classroom

* *Is the room friendly, comfortable, and inviting for teachers and students alike?*

* *Is it properly equipped?*

* *Does the space encourage interaction?*

Materials

* *Will students be provided curriculum material?*

* *Are there enough nice-looking, age-appropriate Bibles?*

* *Will students be provided the materials they need each week?*

Teaching Staff

* *Do you know the number of staff you need, the skills they must bring to the classroom, and how you will recruit and prepare them?*

* *Will teachers work in teams?*

* *Will teachers be expected to teach material or use media they have little experience with?*

* *Will teachers have mentors or someone in the staff structure to whom they can turn for help?*

On Being Practical

Having answered some of the above questions, and maybe even a few questions of your own, what will you have to budget for Sunday School? And how will you cultivate the ongoing support of parish leaders, members, and especially families for what you are proposing to do overall, not just in terms of budget, but in terms of overall purpose and chosen educational model?

A Final Thought

Have you ever thought about how exact the calculations for launch trajectory had to be to get those manned Apollo capsules to the moon in the late '60s and early '70s? If they were off by even a hundredth of an inch at launch, they might miss the moon by hundreds if not thousands of miles over the course of a 250,000-mile flight path. That is, unless they made course corrections and recalculations along the way. It's similar with Sunday Schools. They are established for the long term, and rightly so. But if they are "off" a little to begin with, and make no course corrections along the way, they will miss their mark. That is where good structure (the appropriate model), informed by the proper educational goal of the agency, plays a strong part.

Find someone who shares your passion for the success of your Sunday School and know that God will go with you as you launch your effort to structure your Sunday School appropriately. Be ready to make course corrections along the way. You don't want to miss what you are aiming at—introducing students to Jesus Christ and the saving message in His Gospel.

The Sunday School Classroom

BY DAVID G. EBELING

Wherever it is, it's your classroom! For an hour a week, it is home to a group of children and you, their Sunday School teacher. It may be a small room with a door that closes and you have the space all to yourselves. It may be a corner of a larger room, with other classes occupying the other corners. It may be in the church basement or at the end of the hallway. Your walls may be drywall, a curtain, a sliding partition, or nothing at all.

While the space you occupy is a factor in the effectiveness of your Sunday School classroom, the most important ingredient is not the classroom but God's Word. As the teacher, your passion for God's Word and the Gospel message serve to share that most important ingredient.

* *It's the way you organize and decorate the space you do have.*

* *It's the relationship you establish with the children and their parents.*

* *It's the preparation you do for teaching your lesson.*

* *It's the focus you place on teaching the children about Jesus*

As you reflect on the row of *P*s in the Sunday School garden that follows, you will see ways that each of them helps you with one or more of these aspects: organizing your classroom, building relationships, preparing the actual lesson, and teaching the lesson with a constant focus on the gift of grace through Jesus.

63

Partnership

Sunday School involves a partnership between the congregation and the parents. It is the God-prescribed role of the parents to "train a child in the way he should go, and when he is old he will not turn from it" (Proverbs 22:6 NIV). In becoming a part of a Christian congregation, the parents join with other Christians to do together what one set of parents might not do as well by themselves. Sunday School is organized as one of the ways parents team together to be sure their children hear the Word of God each week and practice applying the biblical truths to their lives.

Your pastor, as the leader of the congregation, called by the congregation to preach the Word and administer the Sacraments, is a significant member of this partnership, one who encourages, trains, clarifies, and supports on behalf of the members of the church. But since your pastor cannot teach all the children and all the adults every week, the partner entrusted with this awesome responsibility and honor is the Sunday School teacher. These teachers step in with enthusiasm, a passion for children, a love of the Word, and a desire to serve.

Pray

I thank my God every time I remember you. In all my prayers for all of you, I always pray with joy because of your partnership in the gospel from the first day until now, being confident of this, that he who began a good work in you will carry it on to completion until the day of Christ Jesus. (Philippians 1:3–6) NIV

This is how St. Paul wrote to his partners in Philippi. He assured them he was praying for them.

Our Lord Jesus tells us to "pray without ceasing." He taught us how to pray by His own example and words. Pray for your class, the students, the lessons, and your teaching. Pray for wisdom, understanding, skill, patience, and joy as you teach the lesson. Pray also for your students, both those who are present and those who are absent, naming them in your heart as you ask the Holy Spirit to take the seeds being planted and grow them into an ever-stronger faith in Jesus as Lord and Savior. Ask the congregation to pray for you and your students.

Most importantly, you teach your students to pray. Start and end each class with prayer. With smaller children, use an echo prayer, in which you say a phrase or short sentence, and the children repeat it. As the children gain spiritual maturity and confidence, they'll read prayers, and eventually become comfortable with contributing prayers from the heart, all because you, the teacher, showed them how to pray.

Place

How you organize and decorate your Sunday School place—your classroom space—sets the tone for the time you have with your learners. When you think about this place as the sanctuary for your mini-congregation, you'll want to make it inviting and meaningful. Start with the way you arrange your furniture. Place tables and chairs (or the school desks) in such a way that you can see the children's eyes when you are addressing them, yet still move about easily to monitor their work.

Strategically place a small table that becomes your classroom altar. Add a piece of fabric for an altar cloth, even changing it throughout the Church Year to reflect the same colors as the altar cloths in church. Add a cross and candles. Stand by this classroom altar when you lead the opening. Face the altar when you pray. Help the children light and extinguish the candles during your devotions time.

Decorate the walls with children's arts and crafts, banners, or meaningful posters. If you can leave the wall hangings up throughout the week, others who use the space will pause to see what the children are learning. If you cannot leave materials on the wall, find a creative way to have them visible while the children are there. If your Sunday School classroom is a day school classroom used during the week by another teacher, find some way, perhaps your altar, that makes the space uniquely special for Sunday School.

Preview

While your class may meet for just an hour or even less on a Sunday morning, you still are a Sunday School teacher all week long, 24/7. In fact, multiply those two numbers (24 x 7), and you are reminded that each of us has 168 hours in a week. Consider adopting a 160-hour rule as you contemplate your lesson for a Sunday morning. Take eight hours off after you teach on Sunday morning, then commit the first of the remaining 160 hours until the next class for preview time.

Before going to bed on Sunday evening, preview the next week's lesson. Open up your materials and glance through all the suggestions for activities and teaching techniques. Identify any craft or project idea that may take extra materials or advanced preparation. Check the title of next week's lesson and focus on the main idea. Read the story narrative from the Bible. Glance over the materials that come with the curriculum. Start memorizing the key Bible verse, even writing it on a 3 x 5 card to carry in your pocket or purse for ready reference all week long.

Look behind you and before you. Consider how next week's lesson ties in with the past week's lesson or how it is part of a sequence that will continue even into the following week. By previewing on Sunday evening, or any convenient time on Sunday, you begin the weekly adventure of making your Sunday School classroom a place where children want to be and where God's Word is proclaimed.

the sunday school classroom

Percolate

The reason you preview next Sunday's lesson 160 hours in advance of teaching it is so the theme, activities, and focus can percolate in your mind all week long. It is amazing how God created our brains so that ideas can reach deep into our memories, finding new connections to an old experience. As you go about your everyday tasks all week long, something will be said or heard or seen that will help you make a connection with your lesson theme.

A news story you hear or see may be on a related topic and give you a way to correlate your Bible lesson to a twenty-first-century event. A teacher guide suggestion for an activity may need some supplies, and you'll more likely remember to find them in your closet or pick them up while shopping during the week.

By the time you get to Sunday morning, the lesson and the way you'll present it is not new; it's been brewing in your brain for a whole week. You will enter your Sunday School classroom with more readiness and more confidence. If you wait until Saturday night to check out the lesson, you will miss this opportunity to let your mind percolate.

Ponder

In the traditional Christian hymn "Praise to the Lord, the Almighty," seventeenth-century hymn writer Joachim Neander penned these words for us to sing, "Ponder anew What the Almighty can do" (*LW* 444:3). To ponder is to take time for intentional, personal deep thought on a particular topic or event.

When you preview early in the week, you read the text of the Bible narrative that is the focus of next Sunday's lesson. As you ponder the text, you might check out some of the cross-references noted in your study Bible. You might come across a theological point that could be discussed or clarified with your pastor sometime during the week. As you ponder, pray again for wisdom and understanding.

A key thing to ponder during the week is the mystery of the love of God. In Romans 5:6–8, Paul sums up the Gospel beautifully:

You see, at just the right time, when we were still powerless, Christ died for the ungodly. Very rarely will anyone die for a righteous man, though for a good man someone might possibly dare to die. But God demonstrates his own love for us in this: While we were still sinners, Christ died for us (NIV).

This is worth pondering. This is why you teach Sunday School.

Props

A prop is any item that is used in a drama or in a teaching environment to help make a point. Props are visual. They can be seen, held, and handled. They help the learner make a connection between what is being said and read. Almost all props are free. They don't come with your teacher guide, but they are all around you in your home, in your closets, garage, attic, or basement. If you've previewed your lesson, you'll likely spot some item during the week that can be used as a prop.

If your lesson is Moses before Pharaoh demanding "Let my people go," pick up a long stick with a crooked end to be a visual of the staff that God told Moses to take with him (Exodus 4:1–5). If your lesson with upper-graders involves Noah's ark, bring in a tape measure and take your students outside to measure just how much of the church parking lot would be taken up if Noah parked his ark there. If you're telling the Christmas story to three-year-olds, collect some baby dolls and towels or small blankets so the children can personally "wrap Him in swaddling clothes."

Use a prop every week. Make finding a prop one of those weekly adventures that helps you prepare your lesson. Children live in a visual world. You'll help them visualize the Bible narrative and better equip them to learn the Bible truths of the day.

Pace

How will you use the brief time you have with your learners? What will you do first? How much time will you spend on the craft? Will there be time for a closing? All of these questions are answered when you deal with "pacing" your class time. "Pacing" is charting out the blocks of time that make up the lesson and then sticking to those times as much as possible.

How long should those blocks be? A child's attention span in minutes is about the same as what their age is in years. So, a four-year-old learner can focus for three to five minutes before becoming bored or easily distracted. The fifth grade class, made up mostly of eleven-year-olds, can typically be kept involved for ten to twelve minutes. Pacing requires that you make a shift or change your style of presenting every so often, depending on age and maturity, during the class time.

Pace your class time so that children experience a variety of activities. Move from a sit-still devotion time to a more active activity time. Try involving the children in retelling the story in a mini-drama after you've asked them to sit quietly when you told it the first time. Use a flannel board to retell a story and invite the children to move the characters and be their voices. Pacing keeps the children involved. Engaged and involved children are less likely to be disruptive.

Practice

For some Sunday School teachers, it's quite natural to be in front of a class, telling a Bible story with accuracy and enthusiasm. For others, it doesn't come quite so naturally. Some Bible stories aren't as familiar as others. Some activities are new. Some crafts can get complex when trying to help a classroom full of students complete them all at the same time. For all these reasons, your personal practice is essential.

Practice telling the Bible story in your own way. The teacher guide will have suggested words to use. You will have read the story directly from the Scriptures as

the sunday school classroom

you prepare and you may read it again to the class—but telling it in your own words is where you often reach your students. Retell the story at your learners' level of understanding. Use puppets to represent the characters, a flannel board to set the scene, or poster pictures that show a sequence of events.

Find an isolated place in your home or car and tell the story out loud. Hearing your own voice is, at first, intimidating. Later, it becomes easier. If you are using props, pictures, puppets, or anything that needs manipulating, try it all out at least once before using it with children. If you're not confident that you'll have names or facts in total memory, prepare a small set of notes you can make reference to while telling the story.

Predict

If it involves kids, something might go wrong, or at least not as planned—and Sunday School involves kids. So plan ahead for the predictable and have an alternative ready for the unpredictable. It will happen. That's part of the adventure of being a Sunday School teacher. The more you predict and are ready for the unpredictable, the fewer discipline problems you will have.

Predict what will distract your learners. If two children typically distract each other, seat them away from each other. If a small child is immature and usually wants to go to Mommy, preplan with the mom how you will handle the options. If you pause to get some last minute materials ready that should have been done before the children arrived, children will quickly fill that pause with unrelated, usually loud and distracting, activities. You can predict that you'll need to call them back to order and you'll waste valuable time doing so.

One thing you can usually predict is that it helps to have an extra pair of hands to assist with details, a pair of eyes to watch for a problem before it escalates, and a pair of feet to run an errand away from the classroom so that you can stay with the children. For these reasons, it is ideal to have a second teacher or a teacher's helper in the classroom. Not only will your teaching partner assist you with the lesson, but he or she might also be able to serve as the substitute if you can't be there.

Present

The first ten Ps listed in this chapter all involve preparation for teaching. Like the proverbial iceberg, much of the teaching role is not seen, but now we get to the actual teaching, that real-time hour when you are with the children. This is the time you present the lesson, pace the timing, predict the unpredictable, manipulate the props, and build relationships with the children.

Start by being present when the first child arrives. Have your materials ready, the room open and bright, the chairs and tables in place, and a welcoming smile for all who arrive. Talk to each arriving child about something in their life: their families, their activities, and their problems. Children will be most attentive during class and more likely to arrive on time when they know that you will greet them personally, know them personally, and genuinely care about their lives outside of the Sunday School hour.

Implement your plan. Have an opening around the classroom altar. Sing those great Sunday School songs and hymns of the Church. Pray with and for the children. Focus on the main idea while you read from Scripture with them, then retell the story using props, help them with their crafts or other activities, and teach them a memory verse. Allow three to five minutes at the end to bring the class to a close. Children value routine and your routine at the end will be to restate the main idea. You know that the first thing the child will be asked by a parent after class is, "What did you learn in Sunday School?" In those last closing minutes, review not only the story, but how it fits into God's great plan to save all of us from sin and death.

Perform

Perform? You mean the teacher needs to perform, as if on stage? Yes! There will be days when your excitement for this role is less than normal because of a stuffy nose, one of your own children had a bad morning, or your mother-in-law is coming for dinner and the menu isn't prepared. But for that one hour: perform. Set aside the rest of your world so the children see only Jesus and your excitement to tell them the Good News.

Performing means there has been a script (lesson plan in the teacher guide). Performing means there are props that need to be ready and in position to be used at just the right time. Performing means the materials for the crafts are ready to use. Performing means you know the Bible story and can tell it—and retell it—with accuracy and enthusiasm. Performing means you wrap up the class with a review, so children leave being reassured that they learned again, or for the first time, that "Jesus loves me, this I know, for the Bible tells me so."

A Parting Word

These are the twelve *P*s in the Sunday School classroom. The more you are prepared, the better your class will go. Some classes will be a delight; some may be frustrating. Through it all, though, be assured that you, in your Sunday School classroom, are sowing the seeds of God's Word into the hearts and minds of the children. You can't make them be Christians. You can't make them have faith. That is the work of the Holy Spirit. You role is to simply, but effectively, plant those seeds of faith in your Sunday School garden.

Love the children entrusted to you by their parents. Enthusiastically open their eyes to see the wonders of the power of forgiveness through Christ. Pray with and for them. Be prepared. Teach each class as if it is the only time a child will hear about Jesus.

Promoting Sunday School

BY LORI AADSEN

Planning for Success

In order to succeed, today's Sunday School needs both growth and outreach. Essentially, this means that you must have a specific plan in place so that your Sunday School reaches the children in your own congregation as well as those in the community. This challenge requires us to keep our efforts true to God's Word, while at the same time relevant to the needs of the families we serve. We should plan every effort in the Sunday School to spiritually nurture and appropriately educate children and their parents. We should strive to keep our programs innovative and exciting because we want children to enjoy their church experiences. After all, the more positive these experiences during their childhood years are, the better chance the church has to keep them connected during their teen years, and into adult life. We must also focus on strengthening the entire family. Most importantly we want children to learn about Jesus as their Lord and Savior. This chapter presents many options for reaching out to families. Consider how you might involve families in your congregation, building your Sunday School at the same time.

The Bible clearly reminds us that God wants parents to be involved in the spiritual training of their children. Deuteronomy 6:6–7 says:

These commandments that I give you today are to be upon your hearts. Impress them on your children. Talk about them when you sit at home and when you walk along the road, when you lie down and when you get up" (NIV).

Parents have more influence than anyone else on their children's faith, yet they need—and want—help. God blesses most Lutheran congregations with vast resources for assisting and supporting parents in the important task of bringing up their children. These are our children! The time is now! With the power of the Holy Spirit we can look to the future with hope and promise!

Finding Direction

Christ, Himself, establishes our relationship with children. We receive firm directives regarding our attitudes and actions toward children in God's Word:

And whoever welcomes a little child like this in my name welcomes me. But if anyone causes one of these little ones who believes in Me to sin, it would be better for him to have a millstone hung around his neck and to be drowned in the depths of the sea. (Matthew 18:5–6 NIV)

Perhaps more than ever before, children need to hear and experience the love of Jesus on a daily basis. Faced with their own sinfulness, children need God's Word of grace for them. Through their Baptism they become members of the body of Christ and ought not be perceived merely as the children of adult members. The baptismal community is an inclusive community. Children are precious gifts from God, uniquely gifted by Him. They need to hear and rehear the biblical story as often as possible, which strengthens both children and adults in saving faith.

A growing number of churches have discovered the importance of a comprehensive effort that includes education and support for parents as well as the education and nurture of children. Sunday School has been the primary vehicle for education and training in the past, but congregations are now realizing one hour per week is not enough. Midweek and other innovative church programs provide wonderful avenues for beginning a total children's ministry with an emphasis on the entire family, one that augments Sunday morning education. But unless we can affect the entire family, including the parents, there is little chance for real change.

The years from birth through grade 6 are the most crucial developmental period of a child's life. Teaching and nurturing should be provided for infants, toddlers, preschoolers, and elementary children with its foundation in a personal, living, and saving faith in Jesus Christ, rooted in the Word. Accordingly, involving parents in their child's Christian education whenever possible strengthens the faith of the entire family!

Many growing congregations realize that the most strategic point of entry for an unchurched family is through effective Sunday School or other children's ministry programs. Search Institute has documented that a major reason for the return of young parents to the Church is a desire to obtain religious education for their children. According to sociologist Wade Clark Roof from the University of California, Santa Barbara, the largest group of former church "dropouts" now returning to church is made up of married couples with children. Ninety-six percent of church members, and seventy-three percent of unchurched adults say they want their children to get religious training, says a Princeton Religion Research Center study. These studies tell us that a solid children's ministry program is a key drawing card for families looking for a church. Not only are parents looking for programs for themselves and their children in the church, they are looking for quality, safety, and a child-friendly atmosphere. These characteristics become essential to attracting and keeping young families.

It is also recognized that a church can serve as a support system for families in the absence of (or in addition to) the extended family. Churches that are most effective in reaching young parents recognize the necessity of having adequate facilities, professional staff, and trained volunteers to minister to children and their parents. Trained professionals will look for every opportunity to make each encounter with children and their parents a moment to nurture faith. As you explore the possibilities in your congregation, consider the following:

Baptismal Classes

Keep track of families expecting a child. Offer a baptismal class taught by the pastor or another qualified person who will be able to explain the meaning of Baptism and the life of a Christian. In this class, offer support by inviting parents to parenting classes, childbirth classes, and cradle roll support. The purpose of this approach is to begin mentoring and supporting parents from the very start. You will also want to inform parents at this time about Sunday School and the other children's ministry programs that are available once the child is old enough. During pregnancy, expectant parents ask many questions about raising a child. Couples who have not been active in church may feel vulnerable, and are usually open to what the church has to offer them. By meeting the needs of these future parents, a prenatal effort can develop a bond between young parents and the church. You will also want to make plans for handling specialized pregnancies (such as high-risk) as well as teenage or adoptive families.

Adopt-A-Grandparent Program

A large percentage of families today relocate frequently. They rarely spend time with grandparents, cousins, aunts and uncles, or other extended family. These homes need the support of an extended church family. Children in this situation often feel alone and isolated. The seniors in your congregation may eagerly participate in Sunday School extra events for building relationships with families. Activities could include crafts, board games, homework, piano lessons, outings, cooking, or reading. This could be an important extended way for your entire congregation to be involved in Sunday School. Grandparents often hold wisdom from life's experiences that children need. They are also able to share their personal faith story to help children see how God guides us throughout our lives.

Family Field Trips

Schedule regular congregational family outings (e.g., picnics, zoo, aquarium, sporting event, theme park, bowling party, skating party, museums, or a family retreat). Always include a time to gather for family devotions and prayer. Showcase your Sunday School in some way during the event as well.

Mom's Groups

Form a group for mothers of young children. Activities could include Bible study, exercise, parenting resources, service projects, guest speakers, fellowship time, and general support. Remember to consider working and stay-at-home mom's schedules. Sometimes a noon meeting serves both groups; or alternate between morning and evening meetings. This is a good place to promote Sunday School as the mom/child's next logical step when the time comes age-wise.

Father's Groups

Offer seminars with guest speakers on the role of the Christian father including Bible study. Provide meaningful activities for dads to build Christian friendships. Also sponsor father/daughter nights or father/son nights and invite fathers to get involved in the Sunday School program.

Teacher Appreciation

Fall and spring offer fantastic times to raise the visibility of your Sunday School and show volunteer teachers your appreciation at the same time. There are a variety of ways to do this:

* *Offer prayers of dedication for staff and families in all worship services.*

* *Introduce the teaching staff and other volunteers in all worship services.*

* *List the teachers' names, a brief bio, and grade level in the bulletin. Be sure to include pictures. Serve lunch or special refreshments after the services in celebration of a new Sunday School year.*

* *Provide a corsage/boutonniere or button for all staff.*

* *Hang Sunday School celebration banners in the entryway, hallway, or narthex.*

* *Select two or three children to briefly share what they like about Sunday School, Midweek, or VBS (have an essay contest with prizes for all entries).*

* *Develop a "Prayer Partner" program where members of the congregation choose a teacher or child to pray for and send cards and small gifts during the year.*

* *Create a slide presentation of past Sunday School classes, programs, and events. Display in the fellowship area or during the lunch.*

All-Year-Long Recognition

Teacher recognition/affirmation is not a onetime endeavor. Here are ways to affirm your staff throughout the year:

Thank-You Gifts/Cards

Simple gifts express appreciation to volunteer teachers. They are symbols of gratitude for faithful service. Get the congregation involved in gift giving not only at the beginning of the school year but all year round. Note: Most parents are eager to assist with gift preparations and cost. Here are a few ideas:

* *Seasonal items (apples, Christmas ornaments, poinsettias, Easter lilies, or candy)*

* *Teacher resource books*

* *Homemade cookies, candy, or other baked goodies*

* *Gift certificates to local restaurants or craft stores*

* *Fresh flowers or potted plants*

* *Mugs, tote bags, T-shirts, pens, pencils, or buttons*

* *Cards or "Thank-you booklets" made by children and/or parents (Be sure to include original children's art, photos, and handwritten notes from children and parents.)*

Sunday School Events

* *Breakfast, brunch, or lunch*

* *Banquet, potluck dinner, or dessert*

* *Family picnic, barbecue, pizza party, or ethnic feast*

* *Short program after eating or a full evening program*

* *Concert or guest speaker*

Teacher Interviews

Arrange for your pastor or another person to interview one or more teachers during a worship service. Keep these tips in mind:

* *Make all teachers feel appreciated and important. (Include Sunday morning and weekday staff as well as the nursery staff!)*

* *Articulate the purpose and benefits of the Sunday School.*

* *Ask these questions: How did you get started teaching? What do you remember about the first class you taught? What is one of your favorite parts of teaching? Why do you still volunteer your time to teach? How have you benefited from being a Sunday School teacher?*

Bulletin/Newsletter Features

Feature a different teacher or department each week in the bulletin, newsletter, or Web site. Include photos, interests, profession, hobbies, and family information of the teachers. Print quotes from teachers about why they enjoy teaching children about Jesus.

Personal Occasions

Send birthday cards to teachers and children—and be alert to other special times (job promotion, anniversary, new baby, etc.).

Treats

Designate one Sunday as Teacher Treat Day. Ask a parent from each class to bring a basket of muffins, cookies, or other treats to their child's teacher. Don't forget to include a thank-you note signed by all the children.

Sunday School Bulletin Board

Create interest in Sunday School with the members of your congregation by placing a bulletin board in a well-traveled area of your church building. Feature a department or age level monthly. Use pictures of teachers and children engaged in activities.

Possible headings could include:

* *"Very Important People"*

* *"Look Who's Teaching Our Kids"*

* *"An Apple for Our Teachers" (Over an apple background)*

* *"People Who Make Things Happen"*

* *"Touching Tomorrow by Teaching Children"*

* *"Focus on Four- and Five-Year-Olds"*

* *"Terrific Third Grade Teachers"*

Touch Points

It has been said it takes seven "touches" for a family to attend Sunday School or worship for the first time. Here are some examples:

1. *Send welcome letters to new families.*

2. *Send home devotions from the Sunday School.*

3. *Create a brochure about your Sunday School and distribute it to the congregation and in the community.*

4. *Distribute invitations to the congregation for Christmas programs and other Sunday School events.*

5. *Send "hands-on" take-home activities designed to involve families.*

6. *Begin parent-teacher conferences.*

7. *Conduct home visits.*

8. *Bulletin, newsletter, and e-mail messages.*

9. *Host a Sunday School Open House.*

10. *Involve parent volunteers.*

11. *Personal phone invitations.*

Be an advocate for Sunday School and all efforts toward children in your congregation. Welcoming children says volumes about how we do ministry in our congregation and community. Congregations that prepare and plan for children are the same churches that welcome those of all ages! If you take bold steps to increase the visibility of your Sunday School, you will see the results ignite the congregation on behalf of children this year!

Special Events

Prayer and Praise Party

What better way to start off the New Year than with a prayer and praise party? This event could be held during Sunday School, Midweek (or after-school program), or in the evening following the New Year's Eve worship service. Plan an hour of crafts, games, devotions, prayer, music, and food. Try some of the following activities:

* *Prayer Chains: Have children write specific prayer requests on strips of construction paper to make a chain. See if you can reach 2,005 (or 2,006) links for your prayer chain! Tear off prayers and lift them up to God during Sunday School in the year 2005/6. Record God's response to prayer in a prayer journal, and then give thanks during the year for answered prayer.*

* *Penny Praise: Ask children to collect and bring pennies to church. Attach*

each penny to double-stick tape mounted on a wall. Pray for missionaries as the chain grows. Continue until you reach 2,000 coins! Send offerings (and pennies) during the month of January to a designated missionary.

* Balloon Thanks: Distribute one large, inflated balloon to each child. As they toss them in the air ask children to name something they are thankful for. Continue, keeping the balloons from touching the ground and giving thanks.

Baptism Birthday Celebration

Celebrate by remembering the Baptism birthdays of children and their families. This intergenerational event gives everyone a chance to celebrate the New Year or new school year with a birthday theme that reminds us of God's grace. The party can be held during Sunday School or following a worship service.

* Cover tables with white butcher paper. Place markers, crayons, streamers, balloons, hats, blowers, and other party decorations on each table.

* Ask families to bring baptismal memorabilia such as a candle, picture, gown, or cap to share.

* Ask families to decorate their table for a birthday celebration.

* Include time for devotions, music, food, and birthday recognition.

* Invite families to decorate birthday cakes or cupcakes.

* Conclude by singing a Baptism song or hymn on behalf of all celebrants.

Take a Trip to Bible Times

Set up a marketplace or town as in Bible times. Reconstruct life as it was 2,000 years ago when Jesus was born. Let children experience the food, customs, dress, and culture of that time.

Faith Family Scrapbook Night

Design a scrapbook making night where families gather to create lasting memories with pictures and other memorabilia. Invite everyone to contribute to the "Faith Family" scrapbook, which will be placed in the time capsule (below) depicting life in your church in the year_____. Conclude with devotions and refreshments.

Time Capsule

Invite everyone to write a brief statement about "What Jesus Means to Me in the Year ____." Include these and the "Faith Family" scrapbook as well as other significant church memorabilia in a time capsule to be opened fifty years from now. Place all items in a stainless steel box or other noncorrosive container. Conduct a brief service to bury the capsule and thank God for His grace and blessings to your congregation over the years.

Celebration Station

Create celebration stations outside your Sunday School area for children to create worship aides to be used during Sunday School worship. Publicize this special Sunday during the month of December asking parents to arrive a half-hour early. Recruit adults and youth to assist children in making praise sticks, joy shakers, and tambourines using instructions found in teacher resource books. Lead the children in a processional using their instruments. Include kids in leading selected parts of Sunday School worship such as music, Bible readings, and collecting the offering.

Thanksgiving

During the month of November ask children and adults to write down one word each Sunday of something that they are thankful for and place it in the offering plate. (Be sure to provide slips of paper and pencils weekly.) On the day of your celebration have children lead the processional during worship carrying brightly colored flags with the words of thanks printed on them (twenty to thirty words per flag). Mention the flags during the prayers, thanking God for His blessings.

Arts Festival

Invite children to express what Jesus means to them through writing, art, drama, or music. Provide an opportunity to celebrate the artistic gifts of children in your congregation. Use the theme: "In the Year of Our Lord ____". Invite children to compose stories, poems, prayers, and essays comparing the Church in the book of Acts to the Church in the present and how the Church may be different in the future. Include original art illustrating the writings as well as music, dance, and drama to round out the event.

Children's Letters to God

Compile letters to God written by the children of your congregation. Younger children can dictate their letter to an adult. Be sure to ask them to illustrate their letters. Publish the letters bound in booklet form. Distribute the booklets as gifts to members and visitors on the day of your celebration.

Promote with Outreach

Service Project

Observe the gifts God has given you by sharing with others. Take children on a local service project to help out at a food pantry, soup kitchen, or homeless shelter. These organizations usually are low on supplies and volunteers during nonholiday times of the year. Begin preparations well before your event by collecting items of clothing, canned food, toys, toiletries, school supplies, and so forth. Coordinate this effort with a local organization for needy children making arrangements for your children to participate in the distribution. Take along tracts that present the Gospel and ask if you can include them with the food or clothing packs you make.

Scavenger Hunt

Organize a scavenger hunt with clues along the way to visit the homes of guests, new members, and shut-ins. Take small gifts made by the children. Conclude by inviting those you visited to a special event at church. (Adults: Ask the pastor or director of outreach for a list of names. Be sure to call ahead for approval.)

Y2Kids Day!

This *Y2K* stands for "You TWO Kids!" Encourage kids to bring a friend to church for this fun day of activities in pairs. Activities could include:

* *Dress alike.*

* *Wear matched crazy socks.*

* *Relay races.*

* *Wheelbarrow races.*

* *One-handed teamwork. (Tie one arm of each pair together. Have the teams assemble a marshmallow tower, frost cookies, decorate friendship cards, and the like one-handed. Time the events and have prizes for the winning teams.)*

"Jesus Loves You" Timeline

Make a timeline of God's saving grace from Adam, Noah, and Moses through the Old Testament. Continue with the birth, death, resurrection, and ascension of Christ. Next, have each child make a personal timeline beginning at his or her birth and Baptism showing how God cares for us today. Also suggest that children depict events in the future knowing God will continue to be active in their lives.

Parades

Assist children in the construction and decoration of a float for a local fair or parade. Have wrapped candy available for throwing with Bible verses attached and invitations to Sunday School.

Puppet Shows

Help older children plan and rehearse a puppet show, musical, or skit to present in a local park. (Be sure to get approval from the proper city officials.) Hand out invitations to Sunday School and worship.

Care Partners

Have children make regular phone calls to share a Scripture passage offering support to shut-ins.

Children's Visitor Packets

Compile a special visitor's packet for children. Include brochures telling about your congregation's Sunday School, devotions, activity pages, crayons, and a tape or CD of children's music.

Children's Newsletter

Publish a quarterly newsletter for children. Include monthly activities, puzzles, word searches, and devotions. Place all visitors on your mailing list.

New Member Welcome

Let children sponsor the children of new members and host a party to welcome them into the church family. Invite new member children to Sunday School and share information about special events. Help children make simple gifts for visitors and go with adults on home visits especially when other children are part of the family. Ask children to make personal invitations to Sunday School and worship.

Celebrate Sunday School!

"We will tell the next generation the praiseworthy deeds of the LORD, His power, and the wonders He has done" (Psalm 78: 4 NIV).

Faith is a gift of God. Through the power of the Holy Spirit, THE CHURCH IS CALLED:

C—Christ-centered teaching/learning environments

* *To welcome, nurture and treasure each child as a unique and precious gift from God.*

* *To proclaim the Gospel to all children in ways that tell and retell God's plan of salvation in Jesus, His Son.*

* *To plan intentionally for Christ-centered teaching/learning environments where children may hear God's Word and respond to His love.*

* *To effectively recruit and equip caring teachers of the faith.*

H—Harbors of hope

* *To proclaim the hope of eternal life to all children.*

* *To celebrate our faith given in the Sacrament of Holy Baptism.*

* *To partner with families as we create atmospheres of hope found in the salvation Jesus won for us on the cross.*

I—Involved congregations

* *To engage the congregation in nurturing, supporting, and enhancing efforts with children starting at birth.*

* To include children, in fulfillment of the baptismal promise, as members and full participants in the congregation, worship, service, fellowship, witness, education, and stewardship.

L—Leaders united in purpose

* To empower congregational boards, committees, and staff to boldly envision dynamic ministry to, for, and with children.

* To foster an atmosphere in the congregation where children, youth, and adults care for one another, and serve Christ as partners in the Gospel both in the community and throughout the world.

D—Dedicated child advocates

* To advocate for the value of every child and their God-given gifts.

promoting sunday school

Basics

well-stocked cupboard

9

The Well-Stocked Cupboard

BY ANITA REITH STOHS

A Teacher's Nightmare

Your primary-level class starts to punch out their leaflet project. Suddenly you realize you just ran out of an essential component of the assembly procedure— glue.

One Saturday evening you find a suggestion in your teacher guide for telling the next morning's Bible story by placing magnet-backed figures onto a metal cookie sheet. You want to try out this new teaching technique the next morning, but there's one problem—you have no magnets and all the local craft stores are closed.

Your lesson went faster than expected, and you are out of teaching ideas with fifteen long minutes left before the children wiggling in front of you return to their parents. You could save the day by having students make quickie, paper-plate stick puppets to use in retelling the Bible lesson—that is, if you had paper plates.

The solution to these three lesson scenarios involves a "well-stocked cupboard" at your teaching fingertips. A well-stocked cupboard provides you with the materials you need to teach your assigned lesson, make simple teaching aids to enhance the lesson, or supply your pupils with the necessary materials needed for reinforcement crafts. This chapter suggests a variety of possible teaching materials, as well as ways in which they could be used.

Ideally, the well-stocked cupboard resides in each teacher's classroom. More realistically there may be only one well-stocked cupboard for your entire Sunday School. It should be housed in the Sunday School Office or another centralized location. In some cases the "cupboard" may travel back and forth from home with you in its own plastic storage container or on a rolling cart.

Our "well-stocked cupboard" list has three levels: Top Shelf Basics, Second Shelf Options, and Bottom Drawer Extras. Pick and choose from the suggested items according to the age of the children in your class, the time in which you have to teach, your classroom budget, and the nature of your classroom area. The Reproducible Page at the end of the chapter contains the full checklist of suggested items.

Top Shelf Basics

Top shelf basics are teaching aids and materials that are useful for most age groups and situations. They include the materials you will normally need to complete leaflet activities or do many of the enrichment activities suggested in your teacher guide. These basic materials could be stored into a plastic tub and easily carried back and forth to a central storage area near the classroom. Top Shelf Basics emphasizes materials that are inexpensive and readily available for purchase.

Second Shelf Options

Second shelf options are useful teaching materials that may not be appropriate for all teaching situations and/or age levels. Teachers should look through the list for materials that their specific class could use on an ongoing basis. Use your teacher guide to choose materials needed for future lessons.

Bottom Drawer Extras

Bottom Drawer Extras include useful materials not likely to be used on a regular basis, but nice to have available for use in special activities or enrichment projects. Many of the items from the Bottom Drawer, as well as items from the two shelves, could be placed on a donation "wish list" distributed to interested parents or congregation members.

Shelf "Inventory"

Top Shelf Basics

Books

Bible

Writing Tools

* Chalk or whiteboard markers and eraser
* Crayons
* Markers
* Pencils (with sharpener, if needed)
* Pens (older children only)

Paper

* Copier paper
* Construction paper
* Ruled writing paper

Other Materials

* Cellophane tape
* Glue sticks
* Newspaper
* Play dough (preschool through kindergarten)
* Scissors
* Washable glue
* Yarn

Equipment

* Hole punch
* Stapler

Second Shelf Options

Books

* Bible atlas
* Catechism
* Children's picture Bible dictionary/encyclopedia
* Children's prayer book
* Children's songbook
* Hymnbook
* Low-reading-level Bible
* Picture Bible

Writing Tools

* Colored chalk
* Colored pencils
* Gel pens
* Glitter glues
* Other crayon options
* Other marker options
* Small-size whiteboard

Paper

* Card stock pieces
* Colored tissue paper
* Poster board
* Copier paper in different colors

Other Materials

* Cotton
* Craft sticks
* Glitter glue
* Stickers
* Fabric trim (especially sequins and ribbon)
* Flannel
* Old leaflets
* Paper or Styrofoam cups
* Paper bags
* Paper plates

Equipment

* CDs
* CD player
* Decorative scissors

Bottom Drawer Extras

Books:

* Children's Bible storybooks
* Children's books that relate to Bible stories

Writing Tools

* Permanent markers

Paper

* Contact paper
* Decorative scrapbook paper
* Roll of shelf paper
* Wallpaper
* Wrapping paper

Other Materials

* Cardboard boxes
* Cardboard tubes
* Clothespins
* Coffee filters
* Cookie cutters
* Crepe paper
* Fabric
* Fabric paint
* Felt
* Fun foam
* Magazines
* Magnets
* Paint
* Plastic lacing thread
* Pipe cleaners
* Pony beads
* Roll of shelf paper
* Round oatmeal boxes
* Sandpaper
* String
* Styrofoam trays
* Tacky glue
* Tin foil
* Velcro
* Waxed paper
* Wooden dowels

Equipment

* Decorative edge scissors
* Metal cookie sheet

Books

The well-stocked cupboard begins with the Bible—the ultimate source of the lesson you are about to teach. Keep a copy of the Bible at hand as you teach, whatever the age of the children in your class. Even young children need to know that the words of the lesson, as well as the Bible passages they hear and memorize, are taken from this book. Refer to an open Bible as you teach, read from it in worship, and set it out as a visual aid to remind the children that the words about God that they hear in your class are taken from the Word of God.

Use a picture Bible to both tell and retell a Bible story to nonreaders, and provide new readers with Bibles written for their reading level. Whenever possible, let the children refer to their Bibles during the lesson. Children's Bible storybooks can be used to teach or review a lesson. Consider putting books for different times in the Church Year into plastic totes that can be rotated in your classroom for use as a pre-session activity. Don't throw away a worn out children's Bible storybook; instead, use figures cut from it to make classroom storytelling puppets.

A hymnbook containing liturgies your congregation uses in worship can be a useful aid to help connect Sunday School and the worship life of your church. As you teach lessons such as the birth of Jesus or Simeon's song as he held baby Jesus in his arms, show how these words of Scripture are used in worship today. Use a children's hymnbook to include music throughout your lesson.

The catechism used for instruction in your church's confirmation program can also be a useful teaching aid as you relate your lesson to sections in it.

Bible reference books, especially those with pictures, are useful for explaining words or concepts that may be unfamiliar to the children in your class. Children's Bible atlases can even become a lesson "storyboard." Use markers to draw Bible characters on small, wooden craft figures and move them over the atlas page as you show the journeys of Bible characters.

Writing Tools

Teachers and students can use chalk, or dry-erase markers, during the lesson time. Draw shapes or words on a board to introduce the story, or stick figures to tell it. Give children colored chalk to use in writing Bible passages or pictures on the board, or to play games that review or apply the story to their lives.

If your class area has neither chalkboard nor whiteboard, bring in a small whiteboard to be used during different parts of the lesson. Pass the board around as you play Bible games that call for writing.

Pencils, crayons, and markers are useful for all elementary grades, though the size and type that you buy depends upon the age of the students in your class. Keep a sharpened supply of pencils for children to use in completing lesson activities, as well as for a variety of lesson applications.

Buy thicker pencils for small children just learning to write. Consider glittery pencils for older children. Colored pencils add interest for completing leaflet assignments, as well as in drawing pictures for lesson applications. If your teaching area does not have a pencil sharpener, keep a small sharpener on hand for emergency classroom use.

Pencils with religious mottos or Bible passages on them serve as a visual teaching aid. Use them in class in conjunction with a particular unit theme, then send the pencils home with students as an ongoing reminder of this lesson. Christian-message pencils also make appropriate gifts for classroom birthdays.

Use crayons, especially with young children. Look for options that add interest to their use. Glitter crayons are popular options, while flesh-toned crayons aid children from different ethnic groups to draw pictures of themselves with the skin color God gave them.

Provide pens for older students. Gel or metallic pens are a popular option for older children to use for writing letters to missionaries, thank-you notes, or invitations to someone to come to a special class or church function. Older children might enjoy using calligraphy or felt-tipped pens for special writing projects.

While not appropriate for very young children, markers are a favorite with most elementary students. Scented, color-changing, or metallic markers are only a few of the many options available to use with your class. Permanent markers can be used by older pupils to draw on Styrofoam or plastic but are not suitable for use with young children. Permanent markers may also be used to draw faces onto small plastic cups to make quick teaching puppets.

Encourage pupils in your class to use writing as a way to creatively review or apply the day's lesson. Children can also write simple prayers or litanies to use in classroom devotion, or retell the lesson through a simple script or "television" interview. Have children work together to write and illustrate a simple book about Jesus' life, death, and resurrection to use with visitors who have not yet heard the story of Jesus' love for them. Older children can make evangelism tracts to give to un-churched family members or friends. All children can make cards to give to the sick or to shut-ins.

Paper

Choose lined writing paper appropriate for the age of the children in your class. Small children in the process of learning to write will do better with wide-lined paper. Consider paper with space at the top for children to add a picture. Use wide-lined notebook paper for older elementary children.

A pack of copier paper provides you with basic drawing paper. Brightly-colored copier paper provides an eye-catching option. Ask your class to draw a picture or cartoon to illustrate a lesson or apply it to their lives. Cut out individual drawings to make stick puppets or dioramas. Glue different shapes together with glue sticks to make classroom posters or bulletin boards. This paper is also suitable for paper-folding activities that can add to an opening or help tell a story.

Construction paper may also be used for drawing paper. Construction paper works best for projects that are glued together to make puppets, bulletin boards, or 3-D craft projects. Have children use construction paper as a background for a picture collage or paper poster or banner. Glitter and marbled paper are options you might choose to use in your class.

Use poster board, either white or in a variety of colors, to add more permanence to class paper projects. A package of heavyweight copy paper can be used for small posters. For mini posters, cards, or bookmarks, buy a bag of multicolored card stock (often used for scrapbooking) to use in making cards or paper crafts. Discontinued wallpaper books available at paint and home improvement stores are also useful for a wide variety of craft projects.

Colored tissue paper is another inexpensive craft material that can be used by all ages for all sorts of activities. Cut tissue paper into small squares and glue on a piece of white paper to make a mosaic cross or other Christian symbol. Wad the squares around the eraser of a pencil to cover the shape with texture. Fill in holes cut into a construction paper shape with tissue paper to make a stained glass window. Tissue paper tucked loosely into plain paper bags dresses them up for use as gift bags.

While newspaper is indispensable for saving the classroom table from getting covered with glue, crayons, and markers, it also is a good source of stories or pictures for older students to use in a classroom collage, poster, or bulletin board.

Other Materials

Top Shelf

Cellophane tape and washable glue are useful for any age, while tacky glue proves preferable when constructing felt banners or projects needing greater sticking power.

Glue sticks work well with paper projects. Yarn is a basic material often needed to complete preschool and primary projects. Yarn can be placed onto a flannelboard as a storytelling technique. Fray yarn to make hair to glue onto puppet creations or a child's "self-portrait" craft project.

Play dough works wonders in keeping preschool children busy when they arrive early, and can be formed into shapes that correspond with the day's lesson theme. Play dough also serves as a backup teaching aid to use with older children, keeping their attention. Mold and move a figure while telling a Bible story or presenting a lesson application.

Second Shelf

Look through your teacher guide for materials needed for upcoming units and include them in your equipment selection. Consider the following additional suggestions in making the choices for your second shelf:

* *Cotton: Glue onto pictures of clouds, or cover cardboard tubes to make sheep.*

* *Craft sticks: Use to make wooden crosses, picture frames, or stick puppets.*

* *Glitter glue: Check your local craft store for different glitter formats to add to Christmas decorations, cards, or other craft projects.*

* *Stickers: Glue stars onto nighttime pictures, attach animal stickers onto creation pictures, or use sticker sets to make paper or felt banners. Draw faces on round stickers and put them onto the ends of craft sticks or onto your fingers for instant puppets.*

* *Fabric trim: Glue ribbon to banners, or use it to hang mobiles. Glue sequins to both Christmas and general projects.*

* *Flannel: Cover a piece of cardboard with flannel, and draw in a background. Glue pieces of flannel to the back of teaching pictures to turn them into flannelgraph figures.*

* *Old leaflets: Reuse classroom leaflets as puppets or class storybook figures.*

* *Paper or Styrofoam cups: Glue or draw figures onto the cup. Glue a craft stick to the bottom of a paper cup to make a stick puppet. Draw a landscape over a large piece of paper and move the cups over it for a table-top drama.*

* *Paper bags: Use markers and/or construction paper, yarn, or fabric to make a variety of hand or tabletop puppets. Adapt large bags into masks, hair, beards, or costumes to use in acting out a Bible time story or lesson adaptation.*

* *Paper plates: Paper plates can be used for a great variety of teaching aids and crafts. Decorate them to make classroom masks or stick puppets. Draw or glue pictures on them to make plaques, then punch holes around the plate for lacing. Cut around and around a plate to make a decorative spiral to decorate with a Bible verse. Cut a paper plate in half and staple it together to make a cone figure; add wings to a cone to make an angel. Place your hand inside the cone to make a puppet, or place several cones together to make a diorama.*

Bottom Drawer Extras

* *Cardboard boxes: Make Bible-times houses, puppet stages, or gift boxes*

* *Cardboard tubes: Cover with construction paper or glue on drawn figures to make stand-up puppets.*

* Clear Contact paper: Cover paper placemats or mosaic pictures made from pieces of colored tissue paper. Place the tissue paper pieces inside two pieces of Contact paper to make a sun catcher.

* Clothespins: Use markers, pipe cleaners and/or fabric scraps to make stand-up Bible figures.

* Coffee filters: Use to hold small materials, or color with drops of watercolor or food coloring to make flowers.

* Crepe paper: Hang from a paper circle to make a day spring windsock.

* Cookie cutters: Have a variety of cutters for use with different lessons and seasons of the Church Year. Use the cutters and dough to make permanent shapes that can be baked and hung as decorations, or trace around the shapes to make paper decorations. Make a stamp pad by placing tempera paint on a paper towel and use the cookie cutters to stamp gift paper.

* Fabric: Let children use fabric pieces for costumes as they act out Bible stories, or glue fabric clothes onto paper bag or clothespin puppets.

* Fabric paint: Write passages and religious mottos on shirts, flowerpots, wooden plaques, poster board, and more.

* Felt: Glue the top around a dowel stick, add a yarn tie, and hang for a banner.

* Fun foam: Make doorknob hangers, refrigerator magnets, or stand up figures. Cover a cross, butterfly, or another lesson-connection shape with small pieces to make a mosaic plaque.

* Magazines: Cut out photos for stick or stand-up puppets or glue multiple pictures together for collages.

* Magnets: Have a set of self-adhesive magnet strips on hand to use to attach paper figures to a metal cookie sheet.

* Paint: Paint pictures illustrating lessons or their applications.

* Paper bags: Draw on them, stamp them, or glue paper and other craft materials onto paper bags to make puppets, gift bags, and more.

* Plastic lacing thread: Add pony beads and fun foam shapes to make necklaces. Use instead of yarn to lace around pictures.

* Pipe cleaners: Use for puppet arms or flower stems. Cover with beads to make simple chrismon decorations.

* Pony beads: Thread over lacing to make necklaces, then add a religious symbol made from fun foam.

* Roll of shelf paper: Use crayons and/or markers to make a Bible scroll storytelling aid. Have children draw along a roll of paper to hang up as a mural or paper banner.

* Round oatmeal boxes: Cover with construction paper to make a large storytelling puppet.

* Sandpaper: Use as a backing for flannelgraph figures, or draw on it with crayons to make a picture or plaque.

* String: Use instead of yarn to hang mobiles.

* Styrofoam trays: Use as a frame for pictures; punch holes around the side and lace with yarn. Cut out a Styrofoam shape and decorate it, or construct a diorama on top of the tray. Place dough projects on trays to dry or to take home.

* Tin foil: Cover cardboard shapes to make props for dramatic productions. Tin foil can also be molded to make simple teaching aids and take-home projects.

* Velcro: Attach Velcro pieces to the back of teaching pictures or shapes to use on a Velcro board made by gluing a piece of polyester fabric onto a piece of cardboard. Or, use Velcro to attach small figures to the tips of a garden glove or make a polyester/Velcro apron.

* Waxed paper: Iron crayon pieces or leaves inside of two pieces of waxed paper to make a "stained glass" picture. Give children a piece of waxed paper to use with classroom cooking projects.

* Wooden dowels: Use for felt banners as well as stick puppets.

Equipment

Consult a school supply list for age-appropriate scissors for your class—safety should be your primary concern. Allow older students to use decorative-edge scissors to cut out paper pieces for a variety of projects. Teachers of younger children should also keep a small stapler and box of staples on-hand to use with paper crafts or to fasten together a fistful of papers for children to take home. The stapler can also turn folded sheets of paper into blank books in which pictures can be glued or drawn to tell or retell a Bible story.

Teachers of younger children will find a hole punch useful for completing projects, crosses, or paper plaques, as well as for lacing projects.

Keep one or two age-appropriate Christian CDs on-hand to play during opening worship, lesson applications, or for children to listen to as they complete a craft or class project.

The Core of Teaching

The suggestions found in this chapter are just that—suggestions. Adapt them to the size of your class and the time in which you have to teach, and most importantly, the age of the students you are teaching. If you have school-age children of your own, be guided by what is in your own family "supply cupboard." Let the kind of materials you buy for your class reflect what you see your children using in school. If needed, check a school supply list for appropriate materials to buy for the age of the children in your class.

In using these materials, keep in mind that the materials and methods you use in teaching is not as important as *what* you teach. All these different options are only means to an end—the clear communication of the Good News that Jesus died for our sins and rose again for the children, for you, and for all people. It is this "Gospel center" that must be at the core of each lesson you teach, giving meaning to Scripture you are presenting, and purpose for the lives of the children who hear it. A lesson without Christ in the center is a moralistic tale with no Christian meaning.

There is one last component to your teaching supply cabinet—a "spiritual drawer." This drawer contains prayer—with which both your lesson preparation and presentation should begin. This drawer is filled with trust that God will be with you in your teaching, as well as with the students in your class who hear your words. The Holy Spirit is there, ready to use the Word of God—spoken and read in your class—as the means to build faith in the hearts of both your students and yourself. It is this "spiritual drawer" that contains the most important source of help and support that you can turn to in preparing and teaching your lesson.

inventory checklist

Resource Cupboard Inventory Checklist

Top Shelf Basics

Books

Bible

Writing Tools

- [ ] Chalk or dry-erase markers; eraser
- [ ] Crayons
- [ ] Markers
- [ ] Pencils (with sharpener, if needed)
- [ ] Pens (older children only)

Paper

- [ ] Copier paper
- [ ] Construction paper
- [ ] Ruled writing paper

Other Materials

- [ ] Cellophane tape
- [ ] Glue sticks
- [ ] Newspaper
- [ ] Play dough (preschool through kindergarten)
- [ ] Scissors
- [ ] Washable glue
- [ ] Yarn

Equipment

- [ ] Hole punch
- [ ] Stapler

Second Shelf Options

Books

- [ ] Bible atlas
- [ ] Catechism
- [ ] Children's picture Bible dictionary/encyclopedia
- [ ] Children's prayer book
- [ ] Children's songbook
- [ ] Hymnbook
- [ ] Low-reading-level Bible
- [ ] Picture Bible

Writing Tools

- [ ] Colored chalk
- [ ] Colored pencils
- [ ] Gel pens
- [ ] Glitter glues
- [ ] Other crayon options
- [ ] Other marker options
- [ ] Small-size dry-erase board

Paper

- [ ] Card stock pieces
- [ ] Colored tissue paper
- [ ] Poster board
- [ ] Printer paper and card stock in different colors

Other Materials

- [ ] Cotton
- [ ] Craft sticks
- [ ] Glitter glue
- [ ] Stickers
- [ ] Fabric trim (especially sequins and ribbon)
- [ ] Flannel
- [ ] Old leaflets
- [ ] Paper or Styrofoam cups
- [ ] Paper bags
- [ ] Paper plates

Equipment

- [ ] CDs
- [ ] CD player
- [ ] Decorative scissors

Bottom Drawer Extras

Books:

- [ ] Children's Bible storybooks
- [ ] Children's books that relate to Bible stories

Writing Tools

- [ ] Permanent markers

Paper

- [ ] Contact paper
- [ ] Decorative scrapbook paper
- [ ] Roll of shelf paper
- [ ] Wallpaper
- [ ] Wrapping paper

Other Materials

- [ ] Cardboard boxes
- [ ] Cardboard tubes
- [ ] Clothespins
- [ ] Coffee filters
- [ ] Cookie cutters
- [ ] Crepe paper
- [ ] Fabric
- [ ] Fabric paint
- [ ] Felt
- [ ] Fun foam
- [ ] Magazines
- [ ] Magnets
- [ ] Paint
- [ ] Plastic lacing thread
- [ ] Pipe cleaners
- [ ] Pony beads
- [ ] Roll of shelf paper
- [ ] Round oatmeal boxes
- [ ] Sandpaper
- [ ] String
- [ ] Styrofoam trays
- [ ] Tacky glue
- [ ] Tin foil
- [ ] Velcro
- [ ] Waxed paper
- [ ] Wooden dowels

Equipment

- [ ] Decorative-edge scissors
- [ ] Metal cookie sheet

BASICS

Special Needs Students

BY LISA KRENZ

Sunday morning dawns and you find yourself walking past the Sunday School classrooms at Redeemer Lutheran Church. First, you see the preschool students gathered in a circle on the floor. Mrs. Jones is leading the children in singing "I Am Jesus' Little Lamb." Most of the children seem to know the words and sing along enthusiastically, but there a few who don't seem to know what they are supposed to be doing.

Mr. Schiller's third and fourth grade class meets across the hall. The children are sitting around the table discussing today's Bible story— except for Billy, he's under the table trying to distracting the others. Just then a loud noise down the hall captures your attention . . .

It is our hope that your Sunday School is filled with many children. Increasing attendance numbers is great news. Those numbers mean that more children are hearing the saving message of the Gospel! Those numbers also represent individual children, each with their own unique gifts and needs. Generally speaking, approximately 10–15 percent of any school-age population is dealing with some type of special learning need. It only makes sense that as the number of children in your Sunday School increases, so, too, the number of children in your Sunday School with special needs will increase. This is indeed a reason for rejoicing. There was a time, maybe not so long ago, that families having children with special needs did not feel welcome at church or in Sunday School. Let's hope this perspective is changing.

Hidden Disabilities

Imagine you are in a situation where everyone else seems to understand the rules of the game and you do not. You look just like the other children in the group, but they appear comfortable here and you feel as if you are in a foreign land. The letters you see seem to jump or turn or look completely unknown to you, but others in the group appear to understand these symbols quickly and easily. Sometimes you get the answer right and then the next time you get the same question wrong. Your pencil moves slowly and clumsily in your hand. You try to say things but the words you want can't be found. You hear your name called often with a stern voice, but you can't quite figure out why. You have a sense that you are doing something wrong, but can't put your finger on exactly what it is. You are just being yourself, but why aren't these people smiling at you?

This is how many children with "hidden" disabilities may feel in a classroom setting. The most prevalent types of special needs are typically not immediately noticeable to the teacher. The majority of students receiving special education services in day schools have been diagnosed with a learning disability. If a student is identified with a learning disability it means that they have average to above-average cognitive abilities, but are significantly delayed in one or more areas of basic reading skills, reading comprehension, writing, math calculation, math reasoning, oral expression (sometimes called expressive language), and listening comprehension (sometimes called receptive language). The delay can be due to a sensory impairment (vision or hearing), cognitive disability, emotional disorder, or environmental or cultural disadvantage. This definition covers a very broad range of learning issues and certainly each child with a learning disability has their own unique set of strengths and weaknesses. In Sunday School, the deficits that become most problematic tend to be reading, writing, and language processing.

It is not uncommon for parents to neglect mentioning their child's learning disabilities to a Sunday School teacher. This lack of communication occurs for many reasons. Sometimes there just isn't the opportunity for parents to speak privately with their child's Sunday School teacher. In other situations parents may fear that the Sunday School teacher will reject their child and not want them to be part of their class. While usually unfounded, this fear is common. Often parents of children with learning disabilities must advocate diligently for their children at school and they don't want to be put in the same position in their church. Whatever the reason, be conscious of the fact that among your students, some will have learning disabilities of which you are unaware.

The other most common "hidden" disability is Attention Deficit/Hyperactivity Disorder or ADHD. While the symptoms associated with ADHD have been described for over 100 years, it has only been during the most recent decades that ADHD has been identified by the medical community as a neurobehavioral disorder. The behaviors that most typically characterize a person with ADHD are the inability to focus, unusual impulsivity, and hyperactivity. These behaviors must be present for more than six months, occur before the age of seven, and be evident in all areas of a child's life (home, school, and play). You may notice that a child with ADHD is easily distracted by self and others, seems to be fidgety and in constant motion, has difficulty with organizational skills, interrupts frequently, has trouble with sustained attention to tasks that require mental effort, and will act before thinking of the consequences.

A child who has difficulty focusing on the task or discussion at hand may also demonstrate weak language processing skills. This will affect his or her ability to follow multistep directions, process abstract concepts, and sequence events. Even though a child with ADHD has average to above-average cognitive abilities, he or she may be delayed in academic or language skills due to a shorter attention span and impulsivity. Typically, children with ADHD are about 30 percent delayed in social skills than their same-age peers. This means that a nine-year-old might have the social skills and attention span of a six-year-old. Children with ADHD may also be highly creative. Some children with ADHD are on medication to manage their ability to focus and control impulses. Not all children take medication when they are not in school. Your students may or may not be on medication for Sunday School.

Some teachers report the biggest struggle when dealing with students with ADHD is behavior management. A combination of positive behavior management strategies and appropriate lesson planning is the most effective way to make Sunday School a successful experience for your student(s) with ADHD. Emphasize and reward positive behaviors. Ignore negative behaviors as much as possible. Be specific and positive when describing desired behavior. For example, say something like, "please keep your hands on your desk" instead of "don't touch your neighbor." Seat the student with ADHD near you. Give nonverbal cues to the student to regain his or her attention. Try a gentle touch on the shoulder or arm, instead of calling out his or her name over and over. Break lessons into shorter segments, vary activities, and use hands-on learning. Provide opportunities for movement throughout your lesson. Keep directions short and check for understanding by asking students to restate directions in their own words. Prepare students for transitions by telling them what's going to happen next, giving them a few moments to shift gears mentally.

Intellectual Disabilities

The terminology in this area is ever evolving. For many years the term *mentally retarded* was the accepted way to describe people whose intellectual abilities were significantly below the norm. While that term is still used, some find that it evokes negative stereotypes; alternate terminology includes *developmentally delayed, cognitive dis-*

special needs students

ability, and *mentally impaired*. Regardless of the term used to describe a person's ability or disability, it is imperative to remember that the person is the important part, not the disability or the term used to describe that one aspect of the person.

Mental impairment is characterized by significant limitations in both intellectual functioning and adaptive behavior. Adaptive behavior refers to a child's ability in the areas of self-care, self-direction, language skills, and social interactions. Children who are mentally impaired may not be developing skills at the same rate as their same-age peers, but they certainly can learn and have meaningful relationships with family, friends, and their Savior, Jesus Christ. Care should be taken to remember that, as with any general term, *mentally impaired* is a broad definition. Children with mental impairments will have a very broad range of abilities. The impact on Sunday School will depend on the individual's own strengths and weaknesses. But generally speaking, a child with a mental impairment will not be reading, writing, or processing abstract language at the same level as his or her same-age peers. You will need to adapt your lesson to meet the individual needs of each child.

Reading

Always ask for volunteer readers. Try not to put students on the spot to read aloud. However, it is not necessary to completely avoid letting students read. Indeed, some students with reading disabilities may want to read. But keep in mind that the pressure to read with no advance warning can cause further stress or embarrassment to a child. Before you start reading, ask for volunteers and assign a section to everyone. This gives you the opportunity to assign a shorter, simpler section when appropriate. It also gives the student a chance to look at their part before their turn comes around.

Other ways to aid reading success include using a highlighter to mark each student's particular sentences. Or when preparing for class, using a copy machine or computer to enlarge print. For longer sections that need to be read aloud, consider reading the passage yourself or tape record the passage using a strong and interesting voice (yours or someone else's). If the class reads the passage in parts, go back to summarize after the reading is complete. Write or draw the key events or concepts where all the students can see them. This turns an auditory activity (listening to other students read aloud) into a visual activity (seeing the sequence of events listed or drawn). Materials at a lower reading level can also be helpful. Even the Bible is available at a lower reading level (e.g., New International Reader's Version). Look for different versions of the Bible story such as the *Child's Garden of Bible Stories, 100 Bible Stories,* or the *Hear Me Read* series from Concordia Publishing House. As you plan your lesson, keep in the back of your mind items that someone in your class may find difficult to read.

Writing

The mechanics of writing can be a stumbling block for many students. Remind yourself and students that you do not "grade" on spelling and grammar in Sunday School. (If you need students to write something perfectly, provide a sample for them to copy. For some students, copying off the board [especially from a distance] is quite difficult. Provide what they need to copy on an index card or scrap paper that can sit on the writing surface next to their paper.) When planning your activities, consider if writing is completely necessary. Perhaps a student could draw a response or dictate their response to you or a helper to write for them. For younger students, consider providing tracing letters made out of sandpaper or other textured paper that children can trace or put paper over to make rubbings. For fill-in-the-blank activities provide a word bank of five words or less. If a student has no writing skills, prepare a name stamp or name stickers (computer labels work well) so that the student can have more independence to identify their own papers.

Language Processing

A deficit in the ability to process and express language is the common denominator of a variety of disabilities. Language-processing deficits are not always as clear-cut or obvious as reading and writing deficits, but they can be more problematic. Judgments are often made about people based on how they communicate. While some students may demonstrate speech problems or even in more severe cases, be completely nonverbal, language goes far beyond the production of speech.

Think about the typical Sunday School lesson. How much of what you teach depends on using language to convey a message? Many times we make the mistake of thinking that a child is not paying attention, when in fact they are not able to effectively process what we are saying. It would be similar to the experience one would have if thrown into a fourth year medical class without ever having had any previous medical instruction. You know they are speaking English and you recognize some of the connecting words, but you have no idea what they are talking about, unless the teacher provides pictures or other clues. You may still not understand a great deal of the medical lesson, but visual images might give you some better clues to aid your understanding. It's not that you can't learn the information, but you need a different approach. The same proves true for children with language-processing problems. It's not that they can't learn the material, but processing the language is difficult. Pictures or other visual symbols provide clues to the message of the lesson and help them understand it.

Remember that the language of the Church can often be very abstract. Words adults use routinely, including *redemption*, *sanctification*, or even *Holy Spirit*, may resemble a foreign language for students with language-processing problems. Find concrete ways to explain abstract ideas. Use visual aids, role play, and hands-on

special needs students

Basics

activities whenever possible. Give directions in short sections, making sure students complete each section successfully before moving on. Write directions or page numbers on the board for students to reference as needed.

The other side of the language coin includes expressive language. This refers to a person's ability to express or communicate with language. Children with deficits in this area often sound as if they are talking all around a subject but just can't "nail it on the head" with the right word. As adults, we sometimes experience that feeling of having a word right "on the tip of your tongue," students with expressive-language issues frequently have this same problem. Thus, their communication often sounds immature for their age. They speak in simple, less complex sentences. But they may have a better understanding of the topic at hand than they are able to express verbally. Think about alternate ways to assess learning. Instead of requiring students to generate a specific word or answer, give them pictures to choose from or provide word choices (depending on age and reading ability). Use a word bank for fill-in-the-blank activities. Allow students to draw responses or develop art projects to demonstrate understanding.

Separate Class or Inclusion?

For many years, children with mental impairments or multiple disabilities were all grouped together in a separate class regardless of age or ability. Today, the best practice involves including children with special needs in the regular Sunday School class with their same age peers. Some situations do arise, however, where it becomes appropriate to form a separate class or to provide individual instruction. When making the decision whether to form a separate, special class or to include children in the regular class, each situation and each child should be considered individually.

One of the most effective ways to include students with special needs is to use a classroom aide. The aide "shadows" the individual student with special needs and helps the student stay on task. The aide may assist with adapting material when appropriate or provide re-teaching when needed. In some cases, the student with special needs may participate for part of the regular class time and the aide may provide individual instruction for another part of the time. Having an aide in the classroom takes the pressure off the main teacher to provide all the support for the student with special needs. It also provides an extra measure of safety; if one adult must leave the classroom, another adult is left with the rest of the children. Most classes benefit from having an extra pair of eyes and hands to answer questions, help with projects, and keep everyone on task. Resist the urge to ask the parent of the student with a disability to be the aide. While the parent certainly knows the needs of their child best, it is also valuable for the student to develop relationships in their church apart from their parents. Parents also need to have the opportunity to participate in adult Bible study, which usually occurs concurrently with Sunday School.

Planning and Teaching Strategies

Some specific instructional strategies were already mentioned in the previous sections on reading, writing, and language. Many teachers find that the strategies they use for students with special needs result in better participation and understanding for all students. It's important for any lesson, but especially when students with special needs are part of your class, to include a variety of activities and approaches. Some students may be strong visual learners; some strong auditory learners, and some may learn best through touch and movement. This proves true whether students have special needs or not. Making your lessons hands-on and actively involving students makes for a better lesson, regardless of the age of your students. Music introduces an invaluable learning tool for all students but may provide an even stronger connection for students with special needs.

Another good practice involves maintaining a predictable routine. Students with special needs sometimes rely very heavily on such predictability. For example, for a student with more severe needs, saying the same prayer every week may be the one part of class where he or she can participate most consistently and successfully. Provide pictures to represent the different components of your class routine (i.e., prayer time, singing, Bible story, project time). Use the pictures to prepare for and manage transitions from one activity to the next.

As you prepare your lessons, always think about those students who might struggle with reading, writing, or language. You may have a visitor next Sunday who has a special need. It's a good idea to keep in mind how you might adapt your activities if such a situation arises. Remember, there is no rule that says that just because it is called Sunday *School* that it has to look just like school. For many students with special needs, school is a very frustrating and scary place. This is not how we want children to feel about coming to Sunday School. As you plan, think about ways you can make your students know how much Jesus loves and cares for them, regardless of their abilities to read, write, and speak.

Parents

Parents know their children better than you do. Parents provide a valuable source of information about their child. As mentioned before, parents of children with special needs may hesitate to share with you at first. They may fear that you will reject their child. They may appear angry or defensive. They may already feel that their child is a burden to you. Emphasize to parents that you are gathering information to help you be a better teacher, not to stigmatize their child. Always reinforce how happy you are that their child is part of your class.

When a child has more involved special needs, make an effort to meet with the parents to develop a spiritual IEP for their child. This is similar to the Individualized Education Plan that a student has in school. Together you and the parents and any

special needs students

Basics

other interested parties (i.e., classroom aide, pastor, DCE, parish nurse) should discuss the child's strengths for learning as well as areas of deficit that will require adaptations. Write down ways that you will adapt the lessons to meet the needs of the child. This meeting provides the ideal time to talk about the parents' goals for their child in Sunday School. What do they hope their child will gain by being in your class? Check to make sure that your goals as teacher match the parents' goals for their child. This is the time to discuss any medical or behavioral questions. Find out if they use strategies or systems that work at home or at school that you should use at Sunday School. If possible, check in with the parents throughout the year and meet again at the end of the year to assess the effectiveness of current strategies.

Specific Disabilities

Entire textbooks are written on the topic of disabilities, so this chapter couldn't possibly address all the specific areas of disability that you may encounter. If you become aware that a student with a specifically identified disability will be joining your class, go to the library or log on to the Internet and do some research. Get information and ideas from special education teachers in your congregation. Find out all you can about the specific disability. Listed below are a few resources to get you started. Then get to know your student. Learn what makes him or her smile. Tell him or her about Jesus. Love them. Share how we are all disabled by the problem of sin and how Jesus came to save us all from sin.

Resources

LeFever, Marlene. *Learning Styles: Reaching Everyone God Gave You to Teach.* Colorado Springs: Cook Publishing Company, 2002. A "must-have" resource for all church/school libraries, this book introduces the four ways people learn and how to identify them, exploring these styles in different Christian learning environments such as in the classroom, during worship, and at home. There are effective activities and methods that can be used with learners of all ages from elementary through adult. Consider also the companion book to this title, *Creative Teaching Methods* by Marlene LeFever, which provides more teaching ideas.

Pierson, Jim. *Exceptional Teaching: A Comprehensive Guide for Including Students with Disabilities.* Cincinnati: Standard Publishing Company, 2002. The author explains the characteristics of seventy-seven diagnoses so that you can identify the challenges, learn how to approach that child, know what teaching and discipline methods work best, and understand what you can expect that child to accomplish. This book is written from a Christian perspective and includes chapters on providing a Christian education, ministering with the family of a student with a disability, and disability-ministry programs.

www.schwablearning.org—While this Web site has a wealth of information about all types of disabilities, it is a great place to find information on learning disabilities and ADHD.

www.ldonline.org—This Web site provides information on learning disabilities and ADHD. It is also a good resource for articles on various sorts of topics regarding special needs.

www.autism-society.org—The Web site of the Autism Society of America; a good place to start research on autism or Asperger's syndrome.

www.blhs.org—The Web site for Bethesda Lutheran Homes and Services, specializing in services and curriculum for people with developmental disabilities.

www.blindmission.org—The Web site for the Lutheran Blind Mission, home of the Lutheran Library for the Blind.

www.millneck.org—Offers deaf ministry information.

www.woodbinehouse.com—Web site for Woodbine House which specializes in publishing books about specific areas of disability.

special needs students

Music in Sunday School

BY JANET MUTH

Make a Joyful Noise

For many children and adults the music they sang in Sunday School is often the most remembered part of their whole Sunday School experience! The songs we sing in Sunday School pass down from generation to generation. Since music makes such a deep impression, it is imperative that the music used during Sunday School be of the highest quality, well-prepared, and full of the riches with which we are blessed as Lutheran Christians.

Sometimes music during Sunday School serves as a warm-up or to attract the children's attention before the "real" lesson. While there is a place for children to sing occasional fun songs relevant to the day's theme, the main use of music in Sunday School should be the same as in the Church at large—to proclaim the Gospel of Jesus Christ. The Lutheran Church has the privilege of a heritage of song second to none! As Sunday School teachers and leaders, we have an exciting opportunity to share the Gospel through great Lutheran hymns.

In some churches, it seems that children and adults sing less and less than in the past. Singing becomes relegated to the intense rehearsal before special events like a Christmas program. Singing can and should become part of our life—not necessarily connected with performing. In worship, singing together combines to proclaim the Gospel and voice our faith together. However, in some settings it has become more commonplace in worship to have a "performer and audience" mindset, rather than congregational participation. Because of this, in Sunday School, we need to encourage children to sing—and thus remember—the truth of Scripture, the joy of our salvation, and the hope of eternal life.

Children process their world differently from adults. The simple reality of being too short to see what is going on in the worship service affects a child's attention span. Coming to church with little knowledge or understanding of the hymns and parts of the liturgy also discourages children in worship. We cannot assume children will "pick up" the order of service or hymns without adults deliberately teaching these elements. Adults in the congregation should also strive to make it clear that each child's participation in worship is important to more than just their mom and dad.

It practically goes without saying that hymns are harder to sing than some of the choruses and quick little songs that some teachers rely upon. But often there are musically appealing aspects to even the more difficult hymns that can be utilized to help motivate students to learn.

In preparing curriculum, lesson plans, and devotional times for Sunday School, a deliberate effort needs to be made to plan and prepare hymns and parts of the liturgy for the children to learn. It is essential that the hymns taught in Sunday School be part of the congregation's repertoire. These same hymns should be sung frequently in worship, to reinforce the learning process. In order to make this happen, coordination during the planning process between pastor, music director, and Sunday School director is essential.

Needless to say, there is an impressive list of things we need to consider when planning and teaching music in Sunday School. This list includes choosing and teaching the highest quality songs from our heritage, choosing and teaching songs that clearly proclaim the Gospel, choosing and teaching music that aides in the memorization of Scripture and basic Christian teaching. In addition, we have the need for coordination and preparation, learning to sing for more than just a performance, and gaining familiarity with hymns and liturgy. We will address all of these aspects of music in Sunday School in this chapter. Also included are suggestions for teaching hymns, liturgy, and songs during the Sunday School year.

As we consider music for Sunday School, the treasures found in our hymnals offer some of the highest quality musical expressions of our faith. Sunday School music can include choruses, antiphons, and simple, repetitive songs, but the core of the music we sing in Sunday School should reflect the musical heritage of our Church. Additionally, these songs and hymns should equip children to participate in the music that comprises the repertoire of the entire congregation. Coordinating the music of Sunday School with the music used in worship reinforces the lessons learned by the children in Sunday School, and connects them to the Divine Service. Advance planning requires anticipating lessons assigned for certain parts of the Church Year.

Familiarity with the stories of Jesus' life, as well as familiarity with certain Bible passages quoted in our liturgy, also helps equip children to participate in worship. As a starting point, a Sunday School could plan one hymn or part of the liturgy to be thoroughly learned each month. A possible scenario follows.

Singing through the Year

September: Psalm 51:15—"O Lord, open my lips . . ."

This phrase sets the tone for the whole year! In Matins, Morning Prayer, Evening Prayer, and Responsive Prayer the service opens with a prayer drawn from Psalm 51:15, "O Lord, open my lips; and my mouth will declare your praise."

This prayer is certainly one all of us as teachers should be praying before we take on the awesome task of teaching the faith to our precious children! It is also an appropriate prayer for the students to pray as we work together in Sunday School. If your congregation sings one of these settings (*LW,* p. 208 or 224; *TLH,* p. 32, 41, or 50); this prayer could be sung at the beginning of the Sunday School hour, as part of an opening devotion, or at the beginning of the lesson.

Week after week, the children pray that the Lord will give them the voice to praise Him. For very young children, this prayer could be introduced—in a very reverent manner—with a puppet who cannot open his own lips, rather the Lord opens them! Older students should learn the Scripture reference in addition to the words of the psalm, and discuss the significance of the prayer they are praying. From this short psalm, a lesson or part of a lesson could be devoted to looking up other parts of the liturgy in the Bible, and memorizing the Scripture reference for each element. This activity helps students become more engaged and curious about the words we sing each Sunday.

October: Psalm 1—"The Man Is Ever Blest" (*LW* 388/*TLH* 414)

Some hymns are close paraphrases of particular psalms. A list of these hymns is found on page 1004 in *Lutheran Worship* or page 187 in *Hymnal Supplement 98.* Older students may benefit from comparing the psalm as found in the Bible with the paraphrase from the hymnal. The short hymn "The Man Is Ever Blest" may be easily learned by "lining out": the teacher sings one line, echoed by the children. If teachers are uncomfortable singing alone, use older students to lead. Like others, this psalm is appropriate for our continued study of God's Word.

November: Matthew 5 (The Beatitudes)— "Jesus Sat with His Disciples" (*HS98* 912).

For many churches, the Gospel lesson for All Saints' Day includes the Beatitudes. This hymn presents the Beatitudes from the Sermon on the Mount in musical form.

**December: Luke 1:26–38 (Annunciation)—
"The Angel Gabriel from Heaven Came" (*HS98* 805)**

For younger children consider teaching only the refrain. Use rhythm instruments to accompany this rhythmically exciting hymn.

Luke 2:1–20 (Birth of our Lord)—"From Heaven Above" (*LW* 37, 38/*TLH* 85)

This hymn, composed by Martin Luther, was written to convey the Christmas story to the children in his family. It is an ideal hymn for children to "act out," with parts for the angel, the angel chorus, the shepherds, and so forth.

January: (Baptism of our Lord)—"To Jordan Came the Christ, Our Lord" (*LW* 223, selected stanzas) or "To Jordan's River Came Our Lord" (*HS98* 816)

Accompanying "To Jordan Came the Christ, Our Lord" with a tambourine helps communicate the rhythmic vitality of this tune to the children.

**February: (Transfiguration of our Lord)—
"Jesus on the Mountain Peak" (*HS98* 818)**

This is another hymn that children enjoy acting out!

March: Psalm 51:10–12 Offertory—"Create in Me"

Found in Divine Service I (*LW*, p. 143) or either Order of Service in *The Lutheran Hymnal* (pp. 12, 22). This text may take some explanation, but the images of clean and dirty are part of the life of any child!

**April: (Resurrection of our Lord)—
"O Sons and Daughters of the King" (*LW* 130/*TLH* 208)**

Another hymn children love to act out. This lesson is traditionally read on the Second Sunday of Easter.

**May: (Ascension of our Lord)—
"A Hymn of Glory Let Us Sing" (*LW* 149/*TLH* 212)**

June: John 6:68—The Common Verse from *Lutheran Worship* Divine Service II, setting 1 or 2

The appealing tunes for both settings of the Common Verse, coupled with the repetition of this part of the service week after week, make these verses easily memorized. The tune for the Common Verse in Divine Service II, setting 2, reflects the "alleluias" in the hymn "A Hymn of Glory Let Us Sing" (*LW* 149/*TLH* 212). The descending musical line provides the opportunity for small children to move with the music: start by standing up, and slowly sit down as the music descends.

July-August: Review

Use the summer months as an opportunity to review songs taught throughout the year.

Singing throughout the Year Again

As you lay out your plan for seasonal songs in advance, continue to build a collection of standard hymns and songs to use throughout the year. Remember, it is not necessary to sing a different song every week! Children benefit from repetition. In addition to the starting point outlined above, other songs for each month could be organized as follows:

September: "Praise God, from Whom All Blessings Flow" (*LW 461 / TLH 644*)

Many congregations sing the "Common Doxology" in worship, at meetings, before or after meals, or at other church gatherings, but we cannot assume that our children will "pick up" this song, without us deliberately teaching it to them. Teach each line of the hymn using pictures drawn by the teacher or students. "Lining out," where students echo back a line spoken or sung by the teacher, is also an effective technique for teaching this hymn. Sunday School students could learn this hymn and sing it at the end of the devotional time or the end of the lesson.

October: "A Mighty Fortress Is Our God" (*LW 298 / TLH 262*)

This hymn contains many images that most children would enjoy drawing themselves, including a fortress, shield, weapon, or even the old evil foe! Be sure to teach at least two stanzas of this hymn, since stanza one ends with a declaration of the strength of Satan. Stanza 2 immediately confesses that we cannot overcome Satan, but that Christ has. Stanza 2 is particularly well-suited for finger play:

With might of ours can naught be done,	*Make "muscle arms" and shake head "no"*
Soon were our loss effected;	*Wave hands, palms down, back and forth*
But for us fights the valiant One,	*Make "muscle arms" and nod head "yes"*
Whom God Himself elected.	*Stretch arms out to make a cross*
Ask ye, Who is this?	*Scratch chin or head as if asking a question*
Jesus Christ it is,	*Big smile!*
Of sabaoth Lord,	*Stretch arms out wide to indicate everything (this requires some prior explanation)*
And there's none other God;	*Again wave hands, palms down, back and forth*
He holds the field forever.	*Point to heaven*

November: "For All the Saints" (*LW 191/TLH 463*)

All Saints' Day is traditionally celebrated on the first Sunday in November. This beloved hymn contains beautiful closing alleluias that young children learn very quickly. "For All the Saints" is also appropriate for the last Sundays in the Church Year, making it a hymn to sing throughout November.

December: "Joy to the World" (*LW 53/TLH 87*)

Based on the second part of Psalm 98, this hymn was originally intended as a hymn about Christ's second coming at the Last Day. Throughout the Advent season we anticipate Christ's second coming.

January: "O Morning Star, How Fair and Bright" (*LW 73*)

This hymn is long, with lots of words, but also filled with images children can picture. Teachers or students can draw pictures of each line as they learn the hymn.

O Morning Star, how fair and bright!	*Picture of the sun, with a cross drawn on it*
You shine with God's own truth and light,	*Bible, with radiating lines of light*
Aglow with grace and mercy!	*Cross with wavy lines symbolizing glowing*
Of Jacob's race, King David's son,	*Manger with Jesus, with pictures representing Jacob and King David in the background*
Our Lord and master, you have won	*Trophy with a heart and a cross on it*
Our hearts to serve you only! Lowly, holy!	*Manger, with star over it*
Great and glorious, All victorious,	*Jesus standing at the empty tomb*
Rich in blessing!	*Treasure chest*
Rule and might o'er all possessing!	*God on the throne over the world*

The descriptions of some of these pictures seem rather complicated, but children often relate to simple pictures that suggest or symbolize the meaning of what they are singing. Discussing the images helps children to understand the meaning of the words they are singing, even if the pictures are stick figures or less detailed line drawings.

February: "Songs of Thankfulness and Praise" (*LW 88/TLH 134*)

Young children will most likely only learn the refrain of this hymn. The word *manifest* is an adjective that means "obvious—clear to see or understand." This little word makes a great starting point for a discussion of the incarnation of Jesus Christ! The rest of the hymn contains themes of the Epiphany season, so it bears repeating for a few weeks.

March: "On My Heart Imprint Your Image" (*LW* 100/*TLH* 179)

This hymn could be taught using simple illustrations or simple finger play. Begin by taking a piece of paper and drawing a dark cross on it with a pencil. Push hard enough so that the pattern is imprinted on the paper. Have the children feel the back side of the paper—how the cross has become imprinted and has actually changed the paper. As you sing, line out the hymn (teacher sings, echoed by students) with the following finger play:

On my heart imprint Your image,	*Put hands on heart*
Blessed Jesus, King of grace,	*Point to heaven*
That life's riches, cares, and pleasures	*Hold up fingers, 1, 2, 3 as you sing the list*
Never may Your work erase;	*Shake your head "no" and take your 1-2-3 fingers and rub them over you heart as if erasing.*
Let the clear inscription be:	*Trace cross on your forehead and heart, as was done at your Baptism*
Jesus, crucified for me,	*Stretch arms out like a cross*
Is my life, my hope's foundation,	*Make a fist with one hand and firmly pound the other palm on the word "foundation"*
And my glory and salvation!	*Extend arms over head*

April: "Jesus Christ Is Risen Today" (*LW* 127/*TLH* 199)

Young students learn to sing the alleluias. Consider having children ring jingle bells on each of the alleluias as a symbol of their joy.

May: "This Joyful Eastertide" (*LW* 140)

In this hymn, the wonderful combination of the musical line and text encourages full body movement for very young students. Start by crouching low. At the words "has sprung to life," jump to a sitting position, with arms outstretched. At the words "had Christ who once was slain," make the saddest face you can make. At the words "But now has Christ arisen, arisen, arisen," smile and slowly start to stand up. At the last line jump to your feet, stretch arms overhead, and dance to the musical treatment of the final phrase!

June: "Lift High the Cross" (*LW* 311)

Try these easy active-learning motions as an approach to this popular hymn:

Lift high the cross,	*Stretch arms into a cross, then lift them high*
the love of Christ proclaim	*Hug yourself, then point to your mouth and extend arms in front of you*
Till all the world	*Put arms in a circle over your head*
adore	*Shake hands above head*
His sacred name.	*Fold hands reverently as if praying*

Used by permission of Hope Publishers.

July/August: Review

Again, the summer months offer an opportunity to review the songs that students learned throughout the year.

Singing the Basics of the Faith

Lutheran hymnody provides a means to teach children the basics of the Christian faith. Through words and music, children learn and retain these teachings. The Six Chief Parts of Martin Luther's Small Catechism each have a corresponding hymn or hymns. Throughout the year, Sunday School leaders could dedicate a period of time to learning each section of the catechism with its corresponding hymn. The section that follows provides hymn and teaching suggestions for each of the Six Chief Parts of the Small Catechism.

Ten Commandments: "Here Is the Tenfold Sure Command" (*LW* 331)

The brief refrain at the end of each stanza offers opportunities for learning, even by very small children. The rhythm of this hymn helps propel it along. At first, one might try saying the text in the rhythm of the hymn, with rhythmic "body percussion."

Creed: "We All Believe in One True God, Father" (*LW* 212/*TLH* 252)

This short hymn could be introduced using simple pictures for each line. Very young children enjoy following the music with their bodies on the last line, stretching high when the music starts high, and following the music down the scale with their hands or bodies.

We all believe in one true God,	*Triangle, with an outstretched hand at top for "Father"*
Father, Son, and Holy Ghost,	*A manger and cross on a bottom point for "Son" and a dove on the other point for "Holy Ghost"*
Ever-present help in need, praised by all the heavenly host;	*Picture of an angel*
All He made His love enfolds, All creation He upholds.	*Cross, with a heart superimposed on it, with a picture of the world on top of the heart*

The longer, chantlike hymn "We All Believe in One True God, Maker" (*LW* 213/*TLH* 251) may be introduced with the children (or teacher) gently waving a beautiful scarf to follow the slow, floating character of the music. The music at the line "He cares for us by day and night" lends itself to a more energetic waving of the scarf!

Lord's Prayer: "Our Father, Who from Heaven Above" (*LW* 431/*TLH* 458)

The minor key of this hymn appeals to children, especially when the teacher models it being sung with hands folded, in a reverent manner.

Baptism: "To Jordan Came the Christ, Our Lord" (*LW* 223)

Accompanying this rhythmic hymn with a tambourine is a great way to energize students and motivate them to rise to its musical challenge.

Confession/Holy Absolution: "From Depths of Woe I Cry to You" (*LW* 230/*TLH* 329)

This is a difficult hymn; it often requires modeling a reverent attitude while being sung. Consider using lining out (teacher sings a line, echoed by students) as the best method to teach this hymn.

Sacrament of the Altar: "O Lord, We Praise You" (*LW* 238/*TLH* 313)

Even in this lengthy hymn the phrase "O Lord have mercy" can be learned by very young students.

These classic Lutheran hymns offer great riches to our children. At first they may seem rather daunting, but as teachers and children sing a stanza every week, they become some of the best loved of the congregation's repertoire.

Great Hymns of the Church

Other hymns that offer concrete images appropriate for children of many ages include:

"Hosanna, Loud Hosanna" (LW 106/TLH 161)

This hymn lends itself to picture drawing. Young children sometimes learn the last line first. "The children sang their praises, The simplest and the best!" Sometimes it is fun for them to NOT sing until the last three words, "and the best." They listen attentively, waiting for their part. In the meantime, they hear the text numerous times.

"Beautiful Savior" (LW 507/TLH 657)

Probably one of the best loved hymns of the Church, it also contains concrete images that the teacher or students can draw.

"Thine the Amen, Thine the Praise" (HS98 867)

This hymn's dramatic setting builds musically as the verse progresses. For older students, consider writing the text of the hymn on the board as a list. Erase one word every time you sing the song, until everything is erased and the verse is committed to memory. Children enjoy singing a song many times with this fun way to memorize.

Many hymns involve long texts, with too many words for young children to learn, especially given the limited time during Sunday School. Hymns with refrains provide a treasury of song for older and younger students to sing together. Hymns with refrains include:

* "All Glory, Laud, and Honor" (*LW* 102/*TLH* 160)

* "All You Works of God, Bless the Lord!" (*HS98* 914)

* "Angels from the Realms of Glory" (*LW* 50/*TLH* 136)

* "Christ Has Arisen, Alleluia" (*HS98* 828)

* "Christ, the Life of All the Living" (*LW* 94/*TLH* 151)

* "I Come, O Savior, to Your Table" (*LW* 242/*TLH* 315)

* "Listen, God Is Calling" (*HS98* 872)

* "Oh, Come, All Ye Faithful" (*LW* 41/*TLH* 102)

* "The Lamb" (*HS98* 822)

* "When I Behold Jesus Christ" (*HS98* 859)

The Gift of Music

Some may ask, if music is not used primarily to entertain or energize the children, is it okay to use the appealing musical qualities of a tune, or allow students to do sometimes rather silly actions? The simple answer is yes! As long as the appeal of the tune or the childlike finger play and acting does not overtake the Gospel proclamation. (It is always the teachers' responsibility to bring the message of the hymn or song to the children's attention!)

Basics

Children love to act, dance, wiggle, and play instruments, but these activities are not the end in themselves, but rather a means to an end. With this approach in mind, even simple songs, antiphons, and choruses can be appropriate after building a core repertoire of hymns sung regularly in worship by the entire congregation, and if they relate to the lesson. Scripture is reinforced and memorized more easily when set to music. Young children benefit from hymns and songs that contain concrete images that help tell a story. Children and adults benefit from repetition and relevance.

The teacher becomes the key to imparting the song of the Church to their students. Many adults are uncomfortable singing alone, or may not know some of the hymns. Sunday School teachers meetings should include singing. As we prepare to teach our lessons, we grow in our own knowledge and devotion. Children are often not as self-conscious or critical of singing as adults. Enthusiastic leadership rates more importantly than concert singing! Accuracy *is* important, however, since the children remember what we give them. Combining classes or having the singing time during a large-group opening or closing devotional time can help consolidate the adult musical resources. If one adult leads the music for the entire group it allows the other adults to participate with the children. This modeling for students is critical. They need to see that singing is part of our life together. As one person leads the group, the voice serves as the primary musical instrument. Children respond to the human voice better than to a piano, so a confident music leader is an important asset. Singing a hymn with a big smile on your face goes a long way in encouraging children to love what they are singing!

It is helpful, but not essential, that a teacher have the hymns and songs the children are learning memorized. Consider singing hymns at home as part of preparation and personal devotion. Teaching the music in Sunday School is not a performance by a teacher. The hymns and songs we prepare should be part of our daily life. Many CDs and tapes are available for listening to hymns.

As Sunday School children learn hymns and liturgy, they aide the congregation by functioning as a choir for the service. This is not to be confused with performing a program! The choir in the Lutheran worship service proclaims the Gospel and aids the congregation's singing. Consider using Sunday School children to sing stanzas of hymns in alternation with the congregation, or to sing the first stanza of an unfamiliar hymn.

Advance planning in cooperation with the pastor and church musician is critical, so that students are well-prepared. A pastor can make a huge difference in the worship life of the young members of the flock by making sure that hymns and liturgy are set well in advance, and that the teachers and musicians know what to prepare. When the music of the service coordinates with the readings and the sermon, children notice and learn to listen closely to find the relationship. Planning ahead is one way to demonstrate that the congregation cares that its children can participate.

Building a core repertoire of the finest Lutheran hymns and parts of the liturgy, preparation, and enthusiasm make teachers of Sunday School music an important part of the imparting of our faith. In this chapter, we've touched on only forty hymns or parts of liturgy. The hymnal is full of more treasures waiting to be shared with our children!

Sunday School Special Events

BY JUDITH CHRISTIAN

P^2—The Power of Programs

Multiply your potential for engaging with children and their families in meaningful ways. Build and nurture intergenerational relationships with children and among congregation families through special programs or events. Programs and events also serve as opportunities for inviting community participation, while raising your Sunday School's profile within your community.

P^2—Purposeful Planning

Subtract last-minute preparations

Every program or event requires a thoughtful process of intentional planning. Doing so allows you to invest in the lives of children and their families, and to watch with wonder and awe the ways God works in and through the ministry to affect children's lives.

Add purpose

There ought to be a driving purpose behind everything! What is the mission of your congregation's Sunday School? Prayerfully consider God's plan for His ministry among the children and families in your community. What is your Sunday School's vision? What are the overall goals for the children? What would children know, be, and do for having been engaged in your congregation's Sunday School? Goals should center around six essential areas for nurturing children's faith and lives as God's dear children: fellowship, Christian education, service, stewardship, outreach, and worship. Every program, event, and activity selected should help realize the vision and achieve established goals for children. Doing so keeps us focused and on track.

Divide responsibilities and share the excitement

The Lone Ranger was a figment of an author's imagination. His character style has no place in the real world of effective leadership. Communicate your vision widely for program development. Surround yourself with those willing to share the load. Recruit a planning team. Identify skills, qualities, or connections necessary to achieve established goals through special programs and events. Invite individuals with these skills, qualities, or connections; and a passion for serving children to participate in the initial process of planning.

Add a follow-up plan

Develop a follow-up plan at the beginning, not at the end. Whether you need to send thank-you notes, file reports, publicly recognize the service and contributions of individuals or groups, or plan a fun-filled ending celebration, make sure you have a fantastic finish!

The sum of all activities is the vision and goals for children

Events that address needs in the community can be great tools to maintain the principles of your vision, if outreach is a main priority. If Christian education is the primary focus, summer camp or events that focus on in-depth Bible study help cultivate faithful habits. If service is your goal, then organized servant events or planned acts of kindness serve to instill this value in children. Planning events for the sake of "doing something" results in valueless blocks of time on already busy calendars. Primary goals give direction and help eliminate distracting activities that cause deviation from the vision, thereby wasting precious time and resources.

Add knowledge about your community

What are the needs of the children and their families? Is there an interest and need for fine arts or performing arts? Is there a need for after school programs? Is the community service minded? What is the racial, cultural, ethnic, and economic make-up of the community? Are there educational needs in the community? Do the research. Also research the past. Look at past programs and events, the rationale for the choice, and the results. Such information provides a basis for change and improvement. In addition, some version of an idea may have been done before, so learn from the work of others.

Multiply mental power

Pray together. Invite the planning team to offer ideas, initially recording and considering all. New ideas build excitement, keep creativity flowing and strong. But new ideas are not always easily embraced. Questions, negativity, reasons it can't be done may catch you by surprise. Respond with the research in mind. Be intentional about defining and refining your purpose. Avoid creating a program or event simply because you can.

Assess program ideas

Assess each proposed idea according to the degree to which it carries out the vision and goals, and addresses identified needs. With the team, list the opportunities presented and any barriers that would need to be addressed to insure that the purpose and objectives of the event or program are achieved. Select only those events or programs that best achieve the vision and goals, offer the greatest opportunity, and can realistically be achieved with the resources at your disposal.

Record the purpose and objectives

Once selected, develop and record the purpose (the reason for having it) and objectives for each. Doing so enables effective evaluation of results. Chart events on a twelve-month calendar (even if you are planning only one or two programs or events for the whole year), so you can assess for any possible conflicts and calendar crowding that would undermine the event or program or deplete your energy. Take time to carefully review your congregation's church and school calendar, as well as any major community or school activities. Select dates and reserve facilities early! Doing so presents more options and allows time to address unexpected challenges.

Thank and dismiss the planning team

Upon completion of the preliminary work, the task of the planning team concludes. Take time to celebrate their significant contribution, thanking them for their service. Enlist their help in identifying program/event team leaders (people who capture the vision and can get the job done). Some members of the planning team may desire to serve in that capacity. Be discerning in your selection. Select and invite each individual with gifts, talents, interests, and connections that match the event for which he or she will be responsible. Remember that some individuals possess the capacity for imagination and creativity while others' gifts lie in implementing the plan. Teams must be comprised of both.

P^2—Positive Preparation

Team participation provides opportunities for potential leaders to try out their skills at leading, planning, and coordinating. These individuals benefit from the team experience, since leadership largely involves helping others achieve their objectives more effectively than they could by themselves. As leaders develop, your Sunday School ministry will continue to grow.

Multiply Your Forces

Involve the entire congregation in praying for the Sunday School and specifically for each event or program. Create as many different types of jobs as possible. Delegate responsibility. This allows almost anyone to find a place to serve with children—some who will be directly involved with children and others who will serve in support roles. Variety gives almost everyone an opportunity to serve according to his or her gifts and interests.

Have the volunteer team leaders recruit their own working teams, using similar guidelines for selection as those used in choosing participants on the initial planning team. Careful selection results in a climate where ideas can be proposed and all members of the team feel free to respond, analyze, and revise. Each team member takes ownership in the plan and is motivated to follow through on assigned responsibilities.

Subtract Confusion and Frustration

A team approach to planning and implementation allows volunteers to maximize strengths and minimize any weaknesses. The unexpected will still occur, but with the full team involved, planners will be less likely to develop an attitude of defeat.

Plan an initial meeting of team leaders

Provide meeting agendas in advance and start on time. Facilitate the meeting to keep discussion focused and moving. You are the vision caster. Spread your enthusiasm with an exciting presentation that is brief, relevant, and visual. Tell the story of the need, the ideas generated by the planning team, and the rationale for the ideas (why important). Providing statistics, references, and other information that substantiates your program ideas can translate into successful programs or events. Be sure each program team has a clear understanding of budget, space, and logistical considerations. Be sure to note your target group, impact on other services (custodians, secretarial staff, Sunday School teachers, etc.), and any future implications.

Organize the task

Avoid handing off program ideas, expecting others to fill in the details. Use to-do lists and timelines to keep yourself on track. Write everything down. Work with team leaders to choose and develop a theme for each program or event. Guide team leaders to, with their teams, determine activities that support the theme and achieve the purpose and objectives of the event. Direct leaders to develop a list of tasks, such

sunday school special events

Basics

as enlisting additional help, gathering supplies, setting up, taking down, cleaning up, and developing promotional materials. Also have leaders work with their teams to establish timelines for task completion and to note who has responsibility for each task.

Create and provide master calendars for each event team leader. Direct them to post established meeting dates, assignments (who is responsible for what and when), and deadlines. Adjust deadlines to prevent "crowding" at certain times of year. Maintain folders for each program or event. Put all material associated with that event in the folder. Create similar folders for each Event Team Leader and instruct them to do the same. At the end of an event, meet with each team and create a note sheet with comments about what went well and what could be improved. Note quantities of food, materials, and any other pertinent information. Place this sheet at the front of the master file for future planning.

Keep in touch with the program/event team leaders both formally and informally.

Schedule a limited number of face-to-face meetings. Use a variety of methods to check progress and to offer support and encouragement, such as e-mail updates, mailbox messages, and telephone conversations.

Formula for Happy Volunteers

You've worked hard to recruit them; you want to keep them. Make their jobs easier and satisfying.

1. *Clearly outline expectations. Communicate the purpose, desired results, and key objectives for each event.*

2. *Provide detailed information necessary for success.*

3. *Return all phone calls and answer all e-mails quickly.*

4. *Meet all deadlines. Never promise performance unless you know you can deliver.*

5. *Know your volunteers and call them by name.*

6. *Listen. Solicit constructive criticism and accept it without being defensive.*

7. *Repent quickly. Admit errors and find solutions.*

8. *Keep meetings and conversation brief and to the point. Demonstrate care and respect for volunteers' time.*

9. *Regularly check progress, offering support and encouragement*

10. *Celebrate their achievements.*

Add the Unexpected

Consider and remove obstacles that might prevent children and families from participating in the program or event. Provide a qualified adult for babysitting the youngest children, organize special children's activities for those children in the age groups not targeted for the event. Serve simple meals at evening events to eliminate family stressors such as preparing and eating a meal prior to attending. Reserve plenty of parking for visitors close to the building. Have parking lot greeters assist families with young children into the building. The registration area should be visible and guides ready to lead people to the location of the event and to the church nursery. Distribute maps of the entire facility that detail the location of bathrooms, nursery, exits, and entrances.

Look at the facility through the eyes of a visitor to ensure that the building climate is one of welcome for children and adults, and that the environment clearly conveys the congregation's beliefs and values.

Include a spiritual dimension at the core of your programs and events by employing devotions, Bible study, a child-friendly lesson, and prayer. Always plan a personal greeting from your pastor and/or other professional church staff. Be sure to include an invitation to participate in worship and other congregation activities. Be sure to distribute Sunday School brochures at every event.

P²—Persuasive Promotion

The best-planned event will not be successful if it is a best-kept secret. Cultivate the desire in people to be a part of the program or event through careful communication.

Multiply Attendance

A multifaceted approach to promotion is necessary to reach your targeted audience. Get publicity out four to six weeks in advance of the event in order to give people time to mark their calendars. Create promotional materials that help your audience visualize the benefits of attending. Communicate special services that will be provided that serve to eliminate obstacles, which might otherwise prevent families from attending.

Use a variety of publicity methods. Brainstorm all the avenues at your disposal to let people know what you're doing and why. Then communicate information regularly and often. Strive to have your Sunday School maintain the highest possible profile in your congregation and community.

Add a Communication Plan

Develop an informative brochure about Sunday School as well as other chil-

sunday school special events

dren's ministry information. Avoid dating your promotional materials; instead develop inserts with the calendar of events and any dated information. Exploit the potential of your congregational Web site—create and update an attractive program/event site. Document activities through photographs and video and display them widely. Create a regular column in your church newsletter featuring an interview or article about event plans, or the experiences of event participants.

Know the audience

Determine from a content standpoint what the audience already knows about your Sunday School ministry and the benefits and opportunities it offers for children and their families. Eliminate terminology that only regular church attendees understand. Use comfortable words readily understood by average readers. Determine reader interests and where they get their information.

Consider the content

Determine who should write the publication. Individuals who know how to put facts and ideas into simple, readable language that attracts attention and holds interest, should do the writing. Communicate the purpose of the event, what will occur, the benefits to participants, and any special accommodations (babysitting, etc.). Content should focus on people, not on buildings. Include quotes from individuals who attended previous events regarding their experiences.

Consider appearance

Make print pieces inviting—attractive to the eye in a quick first glance. Create a common look for all publications. All print and Web site communications should demonstrate quality. Use white space effectively. Break up large blocks of text. Use the dollar-bill test. Place a dollar bill anywhere on a page of the publication at any angle. It should always be touching something other than copy (text). This means that a heading, subheading, photo, or clipart should touch the dollar bill at all times. If this is not the case, the page should be redesigned to avoid long blocks of type, which cause some individuals to reject the page because it looks like too much to read. Use photos to enhance publications. Place your church logo and mission statement on every communication. Also include the purpose statement for your Sunday School.

Consider how people get information

Put promotional information in bulletin inserts, on bookmarks, posters, flyers, and place in your Sunday School and children's ministry brochures. Create an attractive outdoor sign or banner. Check with your city officials to see if you can display banners promoting your event or program around town. Obtain permission to display posters at local grocery stores. Purchase space in local newspapers for notices or advertisements. Contact local radio stations with the information (a certain amount of airtime is often allotted to nonprofit organizations). Urge congregational members to personally invite and bring people from the community—both friends and neighbors.

P^x—Power Unknown

Take time to sit with each team and listen to individual assessments of the event—what worked, what didn't. Invite suggestions for improvement from team members in case the event is repeated. Give each team member, and the leader, the opportunity to share their observations, thoughts, and ideas. Record all comments and add to your event file folder for future reference. Then . . .

Throw a Party!

Celebrate the completion of each event. Thank the planning team(s) and all other contributors to the program or event. Celebrate the blessings God is granting—through your efforts. It is God's power working in us and through the events and programs we plan, and in the hearts and minds of the people who participate, to forward His mission.

Formula for Achieving Objectives

1. Pray!

2. Plan ahead!

3. Know mission of the congregation and its vision and goals for ministry with children.

4. Know needs, community, and past activities.

5. Select initial planning team.

6. Select events/programs for 12 months, attaching purpose and objectives to each.

7. Thank and dismiss planning team.

8. Select event/program team leaders.

9. Team leaders select their own teams.

10. Meet with team leaders and organize the work.

11. Add the unexpected.

12. Regularly touch base.

13. Publicize.

14. Evaluate.

15. Celebrate.

Idea Starters

Children's Education Festival

Help preschool and elementary children and their families experience the excitement of learning about Jesus through hands-on projects and educational booths. Plan this festival as a celebration specifically for visitors. A six-page leaflet, written by Lori Aadsen, detailing this festival is available from The Lutheran Church—Missouri Synod, Children's Ministry.

Children's Reading Program

Solicit donations of Christian books for children, or seek grants, matching funds, and so forth to purchase quality children's books. Set up a twelve-week summer reading challenge for kindergarten through sixth grade children. Keep a 3 x 5 card on file for each child to complete. Add the donated books to the church's library if you have one, or designate a space as a book-lending center for the summer.

(Child's Name)   **Week #**

(Book Title)

What I Learned:

_____

_____

(Parent or Guardian Signature)

Baptism Birthday Party

Plan a birthday party with decorations and a large birthday cake. Invite children and their families who have been baptized throughout the year. Have them bring their baptismal candles and provide candleholders at tables. Prepare a CD, video, or picture gallery containing photographs of the children's Baptism. Lead families in Bible readings, hymns and songs, and prayers. Play the video or CD. Give each family a "Growing Up Baptized" book—a large (8 ½ x 11) blank book (purchased or made by volunteers). Have each family create a Baptism birthday card for their child, adding a note recalling something about the day of the Baptism to put in the book. Provide craft materials for each family to assemble an empty cross to display in the child's room (add Baptism date to the cross). Before serving cake, have families light baptismal candles and sing "Happy Baptism Birthday."

S.O.S. (Service Over Self) Days

Help families to reach out to others and share Christ in church and community. Service activities might include the following: Invite children and their families to assemble May Day baskets with things like fruit, muffins, small plants, candy, and hand-made, Gospel-centered notes. Assemble care kits (soap, shampoo, toothpaste, socks, etc.) by filling gallon size bags with zipper closures, and delivering to local shelters. Prepare simple treats (decorated cookies, pretzels, cupcakes, etc.) and thank-you cards for distribution to various volunteer boards and groups. Take children to nursing homes to play checkers with some of the residents. Rake leaves for single parents or elderly parish members.

Adapted from S.O.S by Audrey Duensing. © 1998. Available from The Lutheran Church—Missouri Synod, Children's Ministry, www.lcms.org.

Hoedown (preschool–grade 2)

Gather children and families to enjoy this festival of music, dancing, and fun! Recruit a square dance caller to lead the group in simple line dances (some physical education teachers have this training); dance the "hokey-pokey"; provide supplies to make quilt squares. Give squares to a group to make them into a quilt for LCMS World Relief. Create a "kitchen band" competition by supplying groups with objects to create musical instruments (pots and pans, spoons, graters, and other kitchen items).

Zippity-Do-Da Days

Throughout the summer, schedule one day a week of special, theme-related activities for children—Bible stories, field trips, arts and crafts, fitness activities, lunch, and snacks.

Seasonal Ideas

Knock, Knock! Trunk and Treat!

Decorate cars and truck beds with a theme in mind (nothing dark or scary!). Invite congregation members to donate wrapped candy to fill the trunks! Have people circle up their vehicles and open up their trunks and hearts to children. Serve a "Cowboy Stew" dinner, after which the children stroll from vehicle to vehicle, receiving candy. Include a sing-along for children, pumpkin decorating, and drawings for attendance prizes donated by local merchants.

Parents Day Out

In early December, invite parents to take a morning to shop or gift-wrap after dropping off their children for a Saturday morning at church. Children enjoy decorating cookies, creating gift-crafts, eating lunch, and then participate in a Christmas play.

Christmas Village

Turn rooms in your facility into Christmas experiences for people of all ages. In the Drama Shop children dress up in simple costumes and present the Christmas story. Take instant-developing or digital photographs of each child in the stable or by the manger. At the Craft Shop provide a low-cost craft for children to make and take. For the Cookie Shop decorate sugar cookies using frosting and sprinkles assembled by the children. In the Video Shop set a schedule for showing a Christmas story video, such as "Red Boots for Christmas." At the Music Shop provide music to which people can sing and play rhythm instruments.

The Great ADVENTure

Assist families in focusing their hearts and minds on spiritual preparations for the celebration of the coming of Jesus. Plan a family project such as an Advent wreath, calendar, or placemats (imprinted with information about Advent, i.e., What is Advent? What is the liturgical color for Advent? Significance of the Advent wreath, etc.) and provide corresponding devotions to use throughout the season. Provide materials for individual craft projects such as angel or star ornaments, serve snacks, teach and sing songs and hymns, and play games all related to your theme.

Giving Station

During Advent, have children assemble gifts that can be given to others in need.

Christmas Breakfast

Recruit the pastor and other men from the congregation who enjoy singing and interacting with young children to entertain and serve children ages 4 and 5 and their guest (each child may bring one guest). Send invitations to all families of young children. Each family should bring a nonperishable food item for admission, which is deposited in a beautifully decorated box or basket. After breakfast each child, along with his or her parent, makes a craft and assembles an Advent calendar/chain.

Family Christmas Program

Select a theme. Choose music and Scripture that supports the theme. Invite families to sign up for different roles in the service: ushering, lighting candles, processional, story presentation, music or pre-service music (solos, family bell or chime choir). Prerecord songs for the service and make available for families to learn at home or in the car. Have each family prepare and bring something with them from home that supports the theme (ornament, altar candle, ribbon for a gift, banner). Items are returned to the family following the program.

For example, if the theme focuses on light, families might bring candles to place on the altar. Sunday School classes prepare age-appropriate carols or an anthem. Rehearse the Saturday before the service and divide families into three groups: songs/music; mechanical (ushers, acolytes, processional); and story presentation. Groups rehearse separately.

Traditional Christmas Programs

Many Sunday Schools share a grand tradition of having the children relate the Christmas story through a Christmas service or program. Avoid the temptation to "over-produce" these programs, adding stress to an already busy time of year. Concordia Publishing House provides Children's Christmas CDs with prerecorded music, scripts, worship service, and Advent and Christmas sermons for such events. These are designed to be complete and easy to use. Help keep the focus on the real message of Christmas—the coming of the Savior.

Consider an alternate time for your program. For many families Christmas Eve may not be the most appropriate time. Perhaps a Wednesday evening Advent service or a Sunday afternoon before Christmas would be more appropriate times for your congregation.

Whenever you schedule your event, recruit a team of volunteers whose sole job is to lead the planning and rehearsal of your program. This allows teachers to concentrate on preparing and conducting their regular Sunday School lessons.

Twelfth Night Party

Choose an evening nearest the feast of the Epiphany. Serve Kings' Cake (bake three jelly beans inside the cake). Those who get the jelly beans are robed as Caspar, Melchior, or Balthazar. An adult is assigned the part of King Herod, while the remaining children are dressed as shepherds, angels, Mary, and Joseph. A baby (or a doll) serves as Jesus. Led by a glittering star, the children and the robed Wise Men lead everyone else in a great and noisy procession. Appropriately position the characters for reenactment of the story from Matthew about the visiting kings. Sing Epiphany songs and hymns. Play Epiphany-themed games. Give each family a printed house blessing and chalk with which to write the Epiphany house blessing on their "lintel."

Midwinter's Night Picnic

Families wear picnic attire and bring their own blankets and picnic dinners as well as desserts or snacks to share with the entire group. Begin the evening with prayer and devotions, eat (provide beverages, utensils, paper products), and lead planned picnic games.

sunday school special events

Winter Beach Party

Use a large indoor facility. Have children bring shorts and T-shirts to change into. Provide several colors of zinc oxide so children can paint their noses upon arrival. Play volleyball with a huge beach ball, jump rope, limbo, dig for hidden items in sand, make summer crafts, and participate in a summer relay. For the relay place six items of beach gear such as sunglasses, flip-flops, goggles, life jacket, inner tube, and a beach towel on the other side of the room. Each person in line must run and get one of the items and put it on, then run back to his or her team. Serve summer-type foods for snacks: corn dogs, snow cones, ice cream treats, watermelon (if available), and lemonade. Include time for devotions focusing on God's Son and His love for us.

Valentine Breakfast

Select a theme such as "Heart-to-Heart" or "Hand-and-Heart," and honor volunteers for their work with children.

Easter Journey

Prepare a multisensory journey for children and their families as they walk the paths that Jesus walked during Holy Week.

Easter Caroling

Take advantage of the more clement weather and carol with children and their families. (Sing Easter hymns and songs that the children know.) Visit congregation shut-ins or community nursing homes. Prior to going, assemble simple gift baskets including cards with an Easter greeting created by the children. Return to the church for theme-related refreshments and games.

Good News Celebration

Invite families for an evening of Good News. The Good News is Jesus and the Easter promise of eternal life. Set up stations for family interaction such as a Craft Station (cross and butterfly ornaments); an Activity Station (families write and post good-news stories about their families; younger children draw pictures); a Fitness Station; and a Dinner Station. Conclude with a family egg hunt and egg-cetera devotions using Easter printed Scripture passages placed in plastic eggs.

Emmaus Walk

Anytime during the Easter season lead children (and their families) on a hike or a walk. Look together for a place where "new life" is emerging. Relate to the resurrection. End with a picnic and tell about the two people who walked (seven miles) with Jesus and then recognized Him at their meal. The men were so excited they ran all seven miles back from where they came to tell others about seeing and talking to Jesus.

Summer Day Camps

Offer day camps that support and encourage children's interests and teach about the love of Jesus. Plan devotions that complement what children are learning. Offer prayers at lunch or snack times. Invite children and their families to worship. Camps might include Fun Fitness—sparks children's interest in a variety of sports or fitness activities; Sports Camps—soccer, basketball, baseball, track; Dynamic Drama—teach how to become a character, build sets, created costumes (non-sewing), develop stage presence; Choral Camp—teach children to read music and singing techniques; Fabulous Fine Arts—nurture creativity through paint, clay, sculpture, watercolor; conclude with a Fine Arts Festival.

Resources

The Lutheran Church—Missouri Synod, District and Congregational Services, Child Ministry, "Children's Ministry Connections" (www.lcms.org).

Concordia Publishing House, resources for Christmas programs (www.cph.org).

The Lutheran Church—Missouri Synod World Relief and Human Care (www.lcms.org).

12